D0843371

EMPEROR NICHOLAS I
OF RUSSIA
THE APOGEE OF AUTOCRACY

EMPEROR NICHOLAS I

A·E PRESNIAKOV

EMPEROR NICHOLAS I
OF RUSSIA

THE APOGEE OF AUTOCRACY
1825-1855

EDITED AND TRANSLATED BY

Judith C. Zacek

WITH

NICHOLAS I AND THE COURSE OF RUSSIAN HISTORY

BY

Nicholas V. Riasanovsky

ACADEMIC INTERNATIONAL PRESS

1974

THE RUSSIAN SERIES / Volume 23

Alexander E. Presniakov **EMPEROR NICHOLAS I OF RUSSIA THE APOGEE OF AUTOCRACY**

Translation of *Apogei samoderzhaviia. Nikolai I* (Leningrad, 1925)

Library of Congress Catalog Card Number: 73-90779
ISBN: 0-87569-053-X
A Catalog Card follows *Suggestions for Further Reading*

Portraits from N.K. Shilder, *Imperator Nikolai I*, St. Petersburg, 1903
Illustrations from P. Artamof, *La Russie historique, monumentale et pittoresque*, Paris, 1862

Printed in the United States of America

ACADEMIC INTERNATIONAL PRESS
Box 555 Gulf Breeze, Florida 32561

CONTENTS

CONTENTS

NICHOLAS I AND THE COURSE OF RUSSIAN HISTORY

Here [in the army] there is order, there is a strict, unconditional legality, no impertinent claims to know all the answers, no contradiction, all things flow logically one from the other; no one commands before he has himself learned to obey; no one steps in front of anyone else without lawful reason; everything is subordinated to one definite goal, everything has its purpose. That is why I feel so well among these people, and why I shall always hold in honor the calling of a soldier. I consider the entire human life to be merely service, because everybody serves.   — *Nicholas I* [1]

The most consistent of autocrats.   — *Schiemann* [2]

Every segment of history, every reign constitutes a problem in continuity and change. And each case is different from all others. Nicholas I's thirty-year-long rule of Russia, "the apogee of autocracy," stands out as a complete and separate entity with a striking unity and logic of its own, which many contemporaries of the emperor, as well as later perceptive historians, such as Presniakov, were quick to emphasize. Yet, this rule, of course, stemmed directly from the evolution of the Muscovite tsardom, more immediately from the development of the Petrine empire, most immediately from the reign of Nicholas I's predecessor, Alexander I. A glance at the historical perspective tends to restore an almost overwhelming sense of continuity. But it should not obscure change.

To put it differently, and to consider only Nicholas and Alexander, the two monarchs represented the Russian version

of general European history. Although brothers, they were
nineteen years apart in age; when Alexander was a boy the
thought of the late Enlightenment held hegemony in the Western world, when Nicholas was growing up Europe was split by
a titanic struggle between Napoleonic France and the old order. One could choose with the Decembrists the French Revolution, or one could defend the establishment. A young
Russian grand duke was much more likely to be found in the
second camp; in fact, because of the milieu and the historical
circumstances he hardly had a choice.

Indeed Nicholas I became the model Russian champion of
restoration and reaction, and the new doctrine of so-called Official Nationality became its canon. The sovereign's utter meticulous devotion to the cause spoke for itself, while Serge Uvarov's brief principles — to which we shall soon return — encap-
sulated successfully the Russian version of the general European ideology of the Right. The thought of the Russian reaction
was, if anything, starker and sharper in outline than its Western
counterparts. Nor should chronology mislead. It might be considered a paradox that Russia was directed in the actual struggle against Napoleon and at the Congress of Vienna by an am-
bivalent and tormented representative of the Age of Reason,
while a dauntless champion of legitimism and reaction ascend-
ed the throne of the Romanovs only in 1825, with the doctrine of Official Nationality formally proclaimed only in 1833.
Yet history is made of just such paradoxes, of responding to
the challenges of yesterday even more than to those of today.

As man and ruler Nicholas I differed sharply from his
brother Alexander I. In contrast to his predecessor's psychological contradictions, ambiguity, and vacillation, the new monarch displayed determination, singleness of purpose, and iron
will. He also possessed an overwhelming sense of duty and a
great capacity for work. In character, and even in his striking and powerful appearance, Nicholas I seemed to be the
perfect despot.

Appropriately, he profited little from most aspects of his

education and always remained an army man, a junior officer at heart, devoted to his troops, to military exercises, to the parade ground, down to the last button on a soldier's uniform — in fact, as emperor he ordered alterations of the uniforms, changing the number of buttons. Participation in the final stages of the war against Napoleon and a happy marriage to Princess Charlotte — Alexandra, after she became Orthodox — of the allied and also militaristic ruling house of Prussia, enhanced this fascination with the army, the roots of which, however, went much deeper than political considerations. And in all other matters, as in military affairs, the autocrat insisted on perfect discipline, order and precision.

Engineering, especially the construction of defenses, was Nicholas's other lasting passion. Even as a child "whenever he built a summer house, for his nurse or his governess, out of chairs, earth, or toys, he never forgot to *fortify* it with guns — *for protection.*" [3] Later, specializing in fortresses, he became head of the army corps of engineers and thus the chief military engineer of his country, probably his most important assignment during the reign of his brother. Still later, as emperor, he staked all on making the entire land an impregnable fortress.

Devotion to defense implied pessimism. In contrast to the organic optimism of the Enlightenment and its expanding vistas, the new intellectual and emotional climate stressed duty, endurance, holding the line, performing one's task to the end. And Nicholas I bore his immense burden faithfully for thirty years, into the catastrophe of the Crimean War. When his diplomatic system collapsed, the weary monarch commented: "Nothing remains to me but my duty as long as it pleases God to leave me at the head of Russia." [4] "I shall carry my cross until all my strength is gone." [5] "Thy will be done." [6] Rarely does one find such congruity among a historical period, character, and convictions.

The government ideology, which came to be known as Official Nationality, was proclaimed on April the second, 1833, by the new minister of education, Serge Uvarov, in his first circular to the officials in charge of the educational districts of the Russian empire. Uvarov wrote to his subordinates:

> Our common obligation consists in this: that the education of the people be conducted, according to the Supreme intention of our August Monarch, in the joint spirit of Orthodoxy, autocracy and nationality. I am convinced that every professor and teacher, being permeated by one and the same feeling of devotion to throne and fatherland, will use all his resources to become a worthy tool of the government and to earn its complete confidence. [7]

The minister proceeded to propound and promote his three cardinal principles throughout the sixteen years during which he remained in charge of public instruction in Russia. In reports to the emperor, as well as in orders to subordinates, he presented these principles invariably as the true treasure of the Russian people and the Russian state. For instance, Uvarov discussed the matter as follows in the survey of his first decade in office, submitted for imperial approval:

> In the midst of the rapid collapse in Europe of religious and civil institutions, at the time of a general spread of destructive ideas, at the sight of grievous phenomena surrounding us on all sides, it was necessary to establish our fatherland on firm foundations upon which is based the well-being, strength, and life of a people; it was necessary to find the principles which form the distinctive character of Russia, and which belong only to Russia; it was necessary to gather into one whole the sacred remnants of Russian nationality and to fasten them to the anchor of our salvation. Fortunately, Russia had retained a warm faith in the sacred principles without which she cannot prosper, gain in strength, live. Sincerely and deeply attached to the church of his fathers, the Russian has of old considered it the guarantee of social and family happiness. Without a love for the faith of its ancestors a people, as well as an individual, must perish. A Russian, devoted to his fatherland, will agree as little to the loss of a single dogma of our *Orthodoxy* as to the theft of a single pearl from the tsar's crown. *Autocracy* constitutes the main condition of the political existence of Russia. The Russian giant stands on it as on the cornerstone of his greatness. An innumerable majority of the subjects of *Your Majesty* feel this

truth: they feel it in full measure although they are placed on different rungs of civil life and although they vary in education and in their relations to the government. The saving conviction that Russia lives and is protected by the spirit of a strong, humane, and enlightened autocracy must permeate popular education and must develop with it. Together with these two national principles there is a third, no less important, no less powerful: *nationality.*[8]

It was for his long service to the three sacred principles that Uvarov was made a count. Still more appropriately, Nicholas I granted him the words "Orthodoxy, autocracy, nationality" as his family motto.

Many poets, writers, professors, and journalists proved eager to echo Uvarov's battle cry, sometimes with a respectful bow in his direction. Stephen Shevyrev, to give one example, followed the minister in 1841, in his analysis of Russia and the West for the first issue of *The Muscovite.* The Moscow professor asserted in his usual ponderous manner:

> But even if we did pick up certain unavoidable blemishes from our contacts with the West, we have on the other hand preserved in ourselves, in their purity, three fundamental feelings which contain the seed and the guarantee of our future development. We have retained our ancient religious feeling, the Christian cross had left its sign on our entire original education, on the entire Russian life. . . . The second feeling which makes Russia strong and which secures its future well-being is the feeling of our state unity, again derived by us from our entire history. There is certainly no country in Europe which can boast of such a harmonious political existence as our fatherland. Almost everywhere in the West dissension as to principles has been recognized as a law of life, and the entire existence of peoples transpires in heavy struggle. Only in our land the tsar and the people compose one unbreakable whole, not tolerating any obstacle between them: this connection is founded on the mutual feeling of love and faith and on the boundless devotion of the people to its tsar . . . . Our third fundamental feeling is our consciousness of our nationality and our conviction that any enlightenment can be firmly rooted in our land only when it is assimilated by our

national feeling and expressed by our national thought and national word .... Because of the three fundamental feelings our Russia is firm, and her future is secure. A statesman of the Council of the Tsar, to whom are entrusted those generations which are being educated, already long ago expressed them in a profound thought, and they have formed the foundation of the upbringing of the people.[9]

In addition to *The Muscovite*, a score or more other periodicals proclaimed "Orthodoxy, autocracy, and nationality" as their articles of faith. They ranged from the fantastically reactionary, obscurantist, and nationalist *Lighthouse* to formal and pedantic government publications, such as Uvarov's own *Journal of the Ministry of Education*. A newspaper with a very wide circulation, *The Northern Bee*, and a similarly popular magazine, *The Reader's Library*, were of particular assistance in disseminating the minister's views throughout the length and breadth of Russia. In fact, until the end of the reign of Nicholas I, Uvarov's brief formula dominated most of the Russian press. Books followed periodicals in spreading the government doctrine. The three sacred principles appeared in many different works, in and out of context, but they became especially common in textbooks and popularizations with a wide circulation. Before long, "Orthodoxy, autocracy and nationality" came to represent much more than Uvarov's attempt at philosophizing, more even than the guiding principles of the ministry of education. The formula expanded to stand for the Russia of Nicholas I.

One attraction of Uvarov's formula was its apparent simplicity. It comprised only three terms, listed always in the same sequence. The content of the doctrine of Official Nationality depended on the meanings and the implications of these key concepts.

Orthodoxy, the first article of faith in the doctrine of Official Nationality, had several basic levels of significance and numerous connotations. In a deep, personal sense it represented, as in the case of Nicholas I himself, the ultimate belief, hope and support of man. Indeed, it was his firm faith in God, Christ, the Divine Will, as revealed in the teaching of the Orthodox Church, that sustained the disappointed and at times desperate emperor in all the trials and tribulations of his hard life. Only Christ, only Orthodoxy, represented for the Russian monarch light, guidance, and salvation in this vale of sorrow and strife.

But, beyond the strictly personal, Orthodoxy also had social functions. According to the proponents of Official Nationality, it was to permeate family life, schools, all of Russian society. In particular, "the entire temple of popular education is to be sanctified by the altar of God, by the cross, and by prayer."[10] The chief function of instruction was to produce right-minded subjects for the Russian empire, and Uvarov discussed this crucial matter in detail in some of his reports to the monarch. Religion and morality appeared prominently in the official orders and regulations of the ministry of education and in other government literature. In fact, right principles and good conduct held the center of attention in the Russia of Nicholas I. The great poet Theodore Tiutchev expressed the official opinion when he observed that in Russia especially the government as well as the Church, had to take charge of human souls. [11]

Autocracy was the second article in the creed of Official Nationality. The law of the land declared: "The Tsar of all the Russias is an autocratic and absolute monarch. God Himself commands us to obey the Tsar's supreme authority, not from fear alone, but as a point of conscience."[12] Or, to quote from the military statutes dating back to the reign of Peter the Great:

> Article 20. Whoever utters blasphemous words against the person of His Majesty, whoever deprecates His intentions and His actions and discusses them in an unseemly manner, he will be deprived of life by decapitation. — Commentary. For His Majesty is an autocratic monarch Who need answer to no one in the world for His actions, but Who possesses power and authority to govern His states and His lands, as a Christian ruler, according to His will and judgment. [13]

Even pithy, legal formulations of autocracy usually included two items: the absolute nature of imperial power, and the link between the emperor and God. For, in the last analysis, God provided the foundation for the authority of the tsar. Most proponents of Official Nationality were well aware of the connection. Such statements as the "heart of the tsar is in the hands of the Lord," Professor Michael Pogodin's special favorite, indicated this awareness. It also found expression in the constant joining of the image of the monarch and of God, one of the most common motifs, in the poetry and the prose of Official Nationality. Typically, in such composite pictures the tsar was represented as the absolute ruler of his great realm yet begging guidance and support from the ultimate ruler of the world, God.

The belief in autocracy was also based on the conviction of the inherent weakness and even wickedness of man and of the resulting need for a strong authoritarian rule over him. As is true of most conservative or reactionary teachings, Official Nationality was a profoundly pessimistic doctrine. Its low estimate of humanity fitted neatly into the Christian framework, if at the expense of neglecting certain basic aspects of Christianity. One of Uvarov's favorite arguments, in his classical research as well as in his other writings, dealt with the fall of man from his initial state of grace, the fact "which alone contains the key to all history."[14] Similarly, Pogodin found everywhere "proofs of the fall of man (which continues in us), of our impaired nature."[15] Other government ideologists generally agreed.

Because men were feeble and perverse, they had to be driven by a benevolent supreme authority in order to achieve desirable social ends. Pogodin combined loud praise of the Russian people, in line with new romantic philosophy, with some reservations on the subject. As early as 1826 he observed: "The Russian people is marvelous, but marvelous so far only in potentiality. In actuality it is low, horrid, and beastly." And he went on to assert that Russian peasants "will not become human beings until they are forced into it."[16] The grammarian and journalist Nicholas Grech proclaimed dogmatically: "Men are not angels; there are many devils among them. Therefore, police, and a severe police, is a necessity both for the state and for all private individuals."[17] He commented as follows on the reign of Nicholas I as contrasted to that of his predecessor:

> Pepper too is required in a salad! Alexander was too meek, replacing during the first years firmness of character with kindness and compassion. This is too good for the vile human species. Now there, I love our Nicholas! When he is gracious, he is really gracious; But when he hits, then willy-nilly they sing: 'God, save the Tsar!' Truthfulness, directness, sincerity, compose, in my opinion, the greatness of any person, especially of a tsar. Why be crafty, when one can issue orders and use the whip.[18]

While social betterment depended on government initiative, the state had a still more immediate and fundamental task to perform: to preserve law and order. The notorious journalist Faddei Bulgarin wrote with unusual conviction:

> It is better to unchain a hungry tiger or a hyena than to take off the people the bridle of obedience to authorities and laws. There is no beast fiercer than a raging mob! All the efforts of the educated class must be directed toward enlightening the people concerning its obligations to God, to lawful authorities and laws, toward the establishment of the love of man in the heart, toward the eradication of the beastly egoism inborn in man, and not toward exciting passions, not toward generating unrealizable hopes. Whoever acts differently is a criminal according to the law of humanity. One who has seen a popular rebellion knows what it means.[19]

Not only did an autocrat embody the ideal form of supreme rule, but at lower levels of government too everything depended on men, not on institutions or legal arrangements. Echoing earlier opinion of a leading writer, historian and conservative ideologist, Nicholas Karamzin, and in particular his emphasis on fifty good governors as the true need of Russia,[20] Pogodin explained the matter as follows:

> There is no institution or law which cannot be abused, something
> that is being done promptly everywhere; therefore, institutions
> and laws are not as important as the people on whom depends
> their functioning.[21]

> One educated, zealous, active superior — and the entire depart-
> ment entrusted to him is, under the system of publicity, aiding
> other departments by its example, organization and training of
> officials. One governor with such qualities — and one fiftieth part
> of Russia is prospering, a second, a third — and all the people can-
> not recognize themselves, they will be the same and yet not the
> same in this general uplift.[22]

Human sinfulness and corruption demanded strong rule.
Force had to be used whenever necessary. Yet the political and
social ideal of Official Nationality was certainly not naked force,
but rather a paternal or patriarchal relationship. Pogodin, the
historian, again spoke for the government:

> There it is, I shall add here, the secret of Russian history, the secret
> which not a single Western sage is able to comprehend. Russian
> history always depicts Russia as a single family in which the ruler
> is the father and the subjects the children. The father retains com-
> plete authority over the children while he allows them to have full
> freedom. Between the father and the children there can be no sus-
> picion, no treason; their fate, their happiness and their peace they
> share in common. This is true in relation to the state as a whole,
> but one notices a reflection of the same law also in its parts: the
> military commander must be the father of his soldiers, the land-
> lord must be the father of his peasants, and even servants in the
> house of every master were called children of the house in the ex-
> pressive old language. As long as this union is sacred and undamag-
> ed, so long there is peace and happiness — as soon as it begins to
> waver, no matter where, there appear disorder, confusion and
> alarm.[23]

The writer Nicholas Gogol made the same point: "Do not for-
get that in the Russian language . . . a superior is called father."[24]

As Pogodin's discussion of "the secret of Russian history" indicated, autocracy found justification not only in religion and in the nature of man, but also in history. Sharing in new currents of thought, the proponents of Official Nationality showed a remarkable awareness of history and the historical approach. Nicholas I read avidly everything dealing with the Russian past, both original documents and secondary works. It was in his reign that chairs of Russian history, as distinct from world history, were established in the universities of the empire, and large sums of money were devoted to the gathering and publication of source materials. Historians and historians of literature, such as Pogodin and Shevyrev at the University of Moscow and Nicholas Ustrialov at the University of St. Petersburg, made important contributions to the development and dissemination of the ideology of the state. Academic writing was supplemented by journalism and by fiction. The age of romanticism proved to be especially favorable in Russia, as elsewhere, to historical drama, novel and story.

The work which presented best the salutary impact of autocracy on Russia was Karamzin's brilliant twelve-volume *History of the Russian State*, interrupted at the Time of Troubles by its author's death in 1826.[25] Karamzin held the position of official historian, and he also won immense favor with the reading public. Repetitions of his theme and variations on it became extremely common in the reign of Nicholas I. Autocracy received incessant praise for binding the Russians together and leading, or driving, them to new prosperity, power and glory. Highly representative of this approach was Ustrialov's *Russian History*, which Uvarov adopted as a textbook in the schools of the empire and which he commended enthusiastically in a report to the monarch.[26]

The entire history of Russia foreshadowed and justified Nicholas I's regime, but its direct line of descent stemmed from Peter the Great. The proponents of Official Nationality, from the monarch himself downward, admired, almost worshipped, the titanic emperor. The historians among them paid special attention to his personality and reign. Pogodin, to take the most interesting example, fell in his youth, if not earlier, under the fascination of the great reformer, this "Russian to the highest degree," the "human God."[27] Later, although specializing in an earlier period of Russian history, he taught a course on Peter the Great's reign, collected documents related to it, and wrote on the subject both as historian and as publicist. The reforming emperor even inspired Pogodin to compose a tragedy in verse, "Peter I", which dealt with a particularly painful episode in Peter's life, his condemnation of his own son, Alexis, to death, and which was written as an apotheosis of the great emperor's sense of duty and of his services to Russia.[28]

The theme of Peter the Great received probably its most brilliant expression in the work of Pogodin's good acquaintance, Alexander Pushkin, and in particular in the great poet's "Bronze Horseman." In this story of a poor, ordinary man, Eugene, who lost his beloved in a St. Petersburg flood, went mad, dared challenge the bronze statue of the builder of the city, and then ran in mortal terror pursued by it, Pushkin presented both the might and the harshness of Peter the Great and of Russian autocracy. While extending sympathy to the unfortunate Eugene, the poet depicted the Bronze Horseman as an infinitely majestic, an almost divine figure, the greatness and permanence of whose work he affirmed powerfully in the introduction. The astounding lines devoted to the emperor, not those describing Eugene, were to remain a treasure of Russian verse. Pushkin's tale is a tragedy, but its composite parts are not evenly balanced: above all rises the autocratic state sweeping on to its grand destiny, undeterred by the obstacles of nature, such as swamps and floods, and impervious to the pain, the sorrow, and even the opposition of the individual, exemplified by Eugene's miserable plight and his pathetic rebellion.

Peter the Great occupied a unique position in the ideology of Official Nationality. He was the founder and a kind of patron saint of Imperial Russia; it was his name that was paired most often with that of the ruling monarch, Nicholas. But there

were other imperial predecessors who also deserved remembrance
and praise, two especially: Catherine the Great and Alexander I.
Catherine merited high consideration because of her achieve -
ments in diplomacy and war, and in spreading enlightenment
in Russia. But Nicholas I disliked her as a person, and the treatment of her in official ideology remained formal and correct
rather than warm and enthusiastic. Alexander I, on the other
hand, was presented as an ideal Christian as well as a great ruler, Nicholas I himself in particular almost worshipping his elder brother. In the literature of Official Nationality, Alexander
was eulogized as the savior of Russia and the world from Napoleon, and as "the angel" who brought humanity into warfare
itself, whose manifestos directed his subjects to return good
for evil, and who spared Paris even though the French had de-
vastated Moscow. Politically he was pictured as a staunch conservative, a great builder and supporter of the legitimist alliance
in Europe.

Yet the riches of Orthodoxy and the traditions of autocracy did not exhaust the content of the official doctrine. It
encompassed still another principle, "nationality." "Nationality," *narodnost*, was at the time and has since remained the
most obscure, puzzling, and debatable member of the official
trinity. While "Orthodoxy" and "autocracy" were relatively
precise terms referring to an established faith and a distinct
form of government, "nationality" possessed no single, generally accepted meaning. It has been most often interpreted as
merely an appendage to "autocracy," an affirmation that the
Russian people were happy, docile, and obedient subjects of
their tsar and their landlords. According to this view, it served
mainly as a propaganda device and possessed no significance
of its own. Indeed, it has been equated by some simply with
the defense of serfdom.

This assessment of "nationality" is largely valid, but incom-
plete. For in addition to its reactionary, dynastic, and defensive connotations, the term also had a romantic frame of reference. And on the romantic plane, "Russia" and "the Russian

people" acquired a supreme metaphysical, and even mystical, importance, leading to belief in the great mission of Russia, to such doctrines as Pan-Slavism and such practices as Russification. Theories attempting to buttress the antique Russian regime met German idealistic philosophy with its dizzying new vistas, restoration met romanticism. It followed logically that the two views of "nationality," which we may call "the dynastic" and the "nationalistic," were in essential contradiction to each other. This contrast and antagonism found expression in the strife between different groups of government ideologists. It was reflected more subtly in the change of position by certain proponents of the state views, while in still other instances the contradiction remained concealed and implicit. In general the concept of nationality accounted for the tensions and conflicts within the government doctrine.

The dynastic view was represented by Nicholas I himself, as well as by most members of his government and his court. It also found expression in such loyal press as *The Northern Bee* with its well-known editors Grech and Bulgarin. The nationalist wing was led by the Moscow professors Shevyrev and, especially, Pogodin, and it included the poet and publicist Tiutchev, as well as numerous participants in *The Muscovite*. The members of this latter group stood close to the Slavophiles, although they remained separated from them primarily by the issue of the nature and role of the Russian state. Moreover, judging by Barsukov's meticulous listing of Pogodin's contacts, nationalist student reactions, gendarmerie reports, and other evidence, they enjoyed considerable support among the Russian public. Indeed, the nationalists possessed, together with their much humbler background, a much wider appeal than the proponents of a dynastic orientation. But romantic, nationalist ideas penetrated even the Russian government, and that on an increasing scale, affecting some of the ministers and other high officials, although they never grew strong enough to replace the essentially dynastic and *ancien régime* outlook of the emperor and most of his aides. The proponents of the dynastic view centered in St. Petersburg, the capital; the nationalists, in Moscow.

The difference between the two points of view came out strongly, perhaps in an exaggerated manner, in the following question of terminology. Whereas Holy Russia was exalted as their key symbol by the nationalists, Bulgarin quoted Count Egor Kankrin, the minister of finance of German origin, as saying:

> If we consider the matter thoroughly, then, in justice, we must be called not *Russians*, but *Petrovians* .... Everything: glory, power, prosperity, and enlightenment, we owe to the Romanov family; and, out of gratitude, we should change our general tribal name of *Slavs* to the name of the creator of the empire and of its well-being. Russia should be called *Petrovia*, and we *Petrovians*; or the empire should be named *Romanovia*, and we *Romanovites*.

And Bulgarin added his own opinion to the minister's suggestion: "An unusual idea, but an essentially correct one!"[29]

Yet, both the representatives of the dynastic orientation and the more nationalistically inclined supporters of the regime, both the Romanovites and the Russians, were in agreement concerning certain fundamental aspects of "nationality." They all emphasized that the subjects of the tsar felt and expressed overwhelming devotion to Orthodoxy and autocracy. Shevyrev, for instance, declared: "I have become accustomed to feel, at the mention of the Russian people, a certain calm, and that not only back in my fatherland, but also all over Europe. The reason is that I indissolubly connect two concepts with the name of the Russian people: unqualified submission to the Church, and the same devotion and obedience to the ruler."[30] Pogodin, in his turn, listed the fear of God, devotion to their faith, and piety among the distinguishing characteristics of the Russian people.[31] Tiutchev declared even more emphatically: "Russia is above all a Christian empire. The Russian people is Christian not only because of the Orthodoxy of its beliefs, but also because of something even more intimate than belief. It is Christian because of that capacity for renunciation and sacrifice which serves as the foundation of its moral nature."[32]

The emphasis on the special character of the Russian people was joined to a general pride in Russia. Nicholas I and his followers stressed the virtues and the glory of the Russians, Russian history, institutions, and language. Language stood out as a vital issue because of its central position in the thought of the age, because of the common acceptance of, and even preference for, French in Russian educated society, and because of the multilingual nature of the Russian state. The emperor wanted the use of Russian in official reports, and even ordered that Russian be spoken at court functions.[33] The government , and especially the ministry of education headed by Uvarov, embarked on a great program of spreading the knowledge of Russian in the non-Russian areas of the empire. Writers and journalists enthusiastically supported the same cause.

To be sure, in spite of its sterling character and peerless language, all proponents of Official Nationality assigned a narrowly circumscribed role to the Russian people. The Russians were to act within the confines of an autocratic regime, to remain obedient and grateful children of their tsar, as well as devoted and heroic soldiers of their officers. Still, even in this estimate of the Russian people differences appeared between those who thought in terms of the traditional dynastic state and those who burned with the new flame of nationalism. The first group tended to be entirely reactionary in its approach: serfdom was defended as an indispensable pillar of Russian society, the education of the tsar's subjects was not to exceed what was proper for their social position, and in general they were to be kept in their place and to remain merely pliant material in the hands of their masters. The nationalist ideologists of the state accepted on the whole the existing Russian order, but they also envisioned some possible modification of it, such as the abolition of serfdom. They wanted to spread education among the masses, to make all people active and enthusiastic participants in the destinies of Russia. They believed in a popular autocracy, in a real union in thought and action between the tsar and his humble subjects. And they came to be opposed to aristocracy, as an obstacle to this union and a class phenomenon which had no place in the true Russian society.

However, the issue on which the two trends within Official Nationality came to diverge the most was the position of Russia in the world. Proponents of the government doctrine thought naturally in terms of a dichotomy between Russia and the West. "The West and Russia, Russia and the West — here is the result that follows from the entire past; here is the last word of history; here are the two facts for the future."[34] But for Nicholas I and most of his assistants this meant battle against revolution in defense of the established order and in full alliance with conservative forces in the German states and elsewhere. For Pogodin, Tiutchev, and some other romantic intellectuals of the Right, on the other hand, Russian "nationality" was even more a promise of the future than a call of the past or a condition of the present. For them Russia expanded to become Slavdom, Russian destiny advancing to the Elbe, Vienna, and Constantinople. A Pan-Slav Russian empire was to replace those of Austria and Turkey which had played out their historical roles. The messianic Russian future called for an adventurous, aggressive, even revolutionary foreign policy which represented the very opposite of the conservative and legitimist orientation of Nicholas I and his government. The contrast between the two views became especially startling in the trying months of the Crimean War, which also marked the end of Nicholas I's entire reign.

Second-rate at best intellectually, Official Nationality proved historically important for a different reason: for thirty years it governed Russia. In particular, Nicholas I's reign reflected in a striking manner both the character and the principles of the ruler, that "most consistent of autocrats."[35] Nicholas's regime became preeminently one of militarism and bureaucracy. The emperor surrounded himself with military men to the extent that in the later part of his reign there were almost

no civilians among his immediate assistants. Also, he relied
heavily on special emissaries, most of them generals of his
suite, who were sent all over Russia on particular assignments,
to execute immediately the will of the sovereign. Operating
outside the regular administrative system, they represented an
extension, so to speak, of the monarch's own person. In fact,
the entire machinery of government came to be permeated by
the military spirit of direct orders, absolute obedience, and precision, at least as far as official reports and appearances were
concerned. Corruption and confusion, however, lay immediately behind this facade of discipline and smooth functioning.

In his conduct of state affairs, Nicholas I often bypassed
regular channels, and he generally resented formal deliberation,
consultation, or other procedural delay. The importance of the
Committee of Ministers, the State Council, and the Senate de-
creased in the course of his reign. Instead of making full use
of them, the emperor depended more and more on special de-
vices meant to carry out his intentions promptly while remaining under his immediate and complete control. As one favorite method, Nicholas I made extensive use of *ad hoc* committees standing outside the usual state machinery. The committees were usually composed of a handful of the most trusted
assistants of the emperor, and, because these were very few in
number, the same men in different combinations formed these
committees throughout Nicholas's reign. As a rule, the committees carried on their work in secret, adding further compli-
cation and confusion to the already cumbersome administration of the empire.

The first, and in many ways the most significant, of Nicholas's committees was that established on December 6, 1826,
and lasting until 1832. Count Victor Kochubei served as its
chairman, and the committee contained five other leading -
statesmen of the period. In contrast to the restricted assignments of later committees, the Committee of the Sixth of December had to examine the state papers and projects left by
Alexander I, to reconsider virtually all major aspects of government and social organization in Russia, and to propose

improvements. The painstaking work of this select group of officials led to neglible results: entirely conservative in outlook, the committee directed its effort toward hairsplitting distinctions and minor, at times merely verbal, modifications; and it drastically qualified virtually every suggested change. Even its innocuous "law concerning the estates" that received imperial approval was shelved after criticism by Grand Duke Constantine. This laborious futility became the characteristic pattern of most of the subsequent committees during the reign of NIcholas I, in spite of the fact that the emperor himself often took an active part in their proceedings. The failure of one committee to perform its task merely led to the formation of another. For example, some nine committees in the reign of Nicholas I tried to deal with the issue of serfdom.

His Majesty's Own Chancery proved to be more effective than the special committees. Organized originally as a bureau to deal with matters that demanded the sovereign's personal participation and to supervise the execution of the emperor's orders, the Chancery grew rapidly in the reign of Nicholas I. As early as 1828, two new departments were added to it: the Second Department was concerned with the codification of law, and the Third with the administration of the newly created corps of gendarmes. In 1828 the Fourth Department was formed for the purpose of managing the charitable and educational institutions under the jurisdiction of the Empress Dowager Mary. Eight years later the Fifth Department was created and charged with reforming the condition of the state peasants; after two years of activity it was replaced by the new Ministry of State Domains. Finally, in 1843, the Sixth Department of His Majesty's Own Chancery came into being, a temporary agency assigned the task of drawing up an administrative plan for Transcaucasia. The departments of the Chancery served Nicholas I as a major means of conducting a personal policy which bypassed the regular state channels.

The Third Department of His Majesty's Own Chancery, the political police — which came to symbolize to many Russians the reign of Nicholas I — acted as the autocrat's main weapon against subversion and revolution and as his principal agency for controlling the behavior of his subjects and for distributing punishments and rewards among them. Its assigned fields of activity ranged from "all orders and all reports in every case belonging to the higher police" to "reports about all occurrences without exception"![36] The new guardians of the state, dressed in sky-blue uniforms, were incessantly active:

> In their effort to embrace the entire life of the people, they intervened actually in every matter in which it was possible to intervene. Family life, commercial transactions, personal quarrels, projects of inventions, escapes of novices from monasteries — everything interested the secret police. At the same time, the Third Department received a tremendous number of petitions, complaints, denunciations, and each one resulted in an investigation, each one became a separate case.[37]

The Third Department also prepared detailed, interesting, and remarkably candid reports for the emperor, supervised literature — an activity ranging from minute control over Pushkin to ordering various "inspired" articles in defense of Russia and the existing system — and fought every trace of revolutionary infection. The two successive heads of the Third Department, Count Alexander Benckendorff and Prince Alexis Orlov, probably spent more time with Nicholas I than any of his other assistants; they accompanied him, for instance, on his repeated trips of inspection throughout Russia. Yet most of the feverish activity of the gendarmes seemed to be to no purpose. Endless investigation of subversion, stimulated by the monarch's own suspiciousness, revealed very little. Even the most important radical group uncovered during the reign, the Petrashevtsy, fell victim not to the gendarmery but to its great rival, the ordinary police, which continued to be part of the Ministry of the Interior.

The desire to control in detail the lives and thoughts of the people and above all to prevent subversion guided also the policies of the Ministry of Education, and in fact served as an inspiration for the entire reign. As in the building of fortresses the emphasis was defensive: to hold fast against the enemy and to prevent his penetration. The sovereign himself worked indefatigably at shoring up the defenses. He paid the most painstaking attention to the huge and difficult business of government, did his own inspecting of the country, rushed to meet all kinds of emergencies, from cholera epidemics and riots to rebellions in military settlements, and bestowed special care on the army. Beyond all that, and beyond even the needs of defense, he wanted to follow the sacred principle of autocracy, to be a true father of his people, concerned with their daily lives, hopes, and fears.

Education continued to attract the attention of the emperor and his assistants. During the thirty years of Official Nationality, with Uvarov himself serving as minister of education from 1833 to 1849, the government tried to centralize and standardize education; to limit the individual's schooling according to his social background, so that each person would remain in his assigned place in life; to foster the official ideology exclusively; and, especially, to eliminate every trace or possibility of intellectual opposition or subversion.

As to centralization and standardization, Nicholas I and his associates did everything in their power to introduce absolute order and regularity into the educational system of Russia. The state even extended its minute control to private schools and indeed to education in the home. By a series of laws and rules issued in 1833-35, private institutions, which were not to increase in number in the future except where public schooling was not available, received regulations and instructions from central authorities, while inspector were appointed to assure their compliance. "They had to submit to the law of unity which formed the foundation of the reign."[38] Home education came under state influence through rigid government control of teachers: Russian private tutors began to be considered state employees, subject to appropriate examinations and enjoying the same pensions and awards as other comparable officials; at the same time the government strictly prohibited the hiring of foreign instructors who did not possess the requisite certificates testifying to academic competence and exemplary moral character. Nicholas I himself led the way in supervising and inspecting schools in Russia, and the emperor's assistants followed his example.

The restrictive policies of the Ministry of Education resulted logically from its social views and aims. In order to assure that each class of Russians obtained only "that part which it needs from the general treasury of enlightenment," the government resorted to increased tuition rates and to such requirements as special certificates of leave that pupils belonging to the lower layers of society had to obtain from their village or town before they could attend secondary school. Members of the upper class, by contrast, received inducements to continue their education, many boarding schools for the gentry being created for that purpose. Ideally, in the government scheme of things − and reality failed to live up to the ideal − children of peasants and of lower classes in general were to attend only parish schools or other schools of similar educational level, students of middle-class origin were to study in the district schools, while secondary schools and universities catered primarily, although not exclusively, to the gentry. Special efforts were made throughout the reign to restrict the education of the serfs to elementary and "useful" subjects. Schools for girls, which were under the patronage of Empress Dowager Mary and the jurisdiction of the Fourth Department of His Majesty's Own Chancery, served the same aims as those for boys.

The inculcation of the true doctrine, that of Official Nationality, and a relentless struggle against all pernicious ideas constituted, of course, essential activities of the Ministry of Education. Only officially approved views received endorsement, and they had to be accepted without question rather than discussed. Teachers and students, lectures and books were generally suspect and required a watchful eye. In 1834 full-time inspectors were introduced into universities to keep vigil over the behavior of students outside the classroom. Education and knowledge, in the estimate of the emperor and his associates, could easily become subversion. With the revolutionary year of 1848, unrelieved repression set in. "Neither blame, nor praise is compatible with the dignity of the government or with the order which fortunately exists among us; one must obey and keep one's thoughts to oneself."[39]

Still, the government of Nicholas I made some significant contributions to the development of education in Russia. Thus, it should be noted that the Ministry of Education spent large sums to provide new buildings, laboratories, and libraries, and other aids to scholarship such as the excellent Pulkovo observatory; that teachers' salaries were substantially increased — extraordinarily increased in the case of professors, according to the University Statute of 1835; that, in general, the government of Nicholas I showed a commendable interest in the physical plant necessary for education and in the material well-being of those engaged in instruction. Nor was quality neglected. Uvarov in particular did much to raise educational and scholarly standards in Russia in the sixteen years during which he headed the ministry. Especially important proved to be the establishment of many new chairs, the corresponding opening up of numerous new fields of learning in the universities of the empire, and the practice of sending promising young Russian scholars abroad for extended training. The Russian educational system, with all its fundamental flaws, came to emphasize academic thoroughness and high standards. Indeed, the government utilized the standards to make education more exclusive at all levels of schooling. Following the Polish rebellion, the Polish University of Vilno was closed; in 1833 a Russian university was opened in Kiev instead. The government of Nicholas I created no other new universities, but it did establish a number of technical and "practical" institutions of higher learning, such as a technological institute, a school of jurisprudence, and a school of architecture, as well as schools of arts and crafts, agriculture, and veterinary medicine.

But, demanding and decisive in little things, Nicholas I could not even approach major reform. Serfdom provided the crucial issue. The emperor personally disapproved of that institution: in the army and in the country at large he saw only too well the misery it produced, and he remained constantly apprehensive of the danger of insurrection; also, the autocrat had no sympathy for aristocratic privilege when it clashed with the interests of the state. Yet, as he explained the matter in 1842 in the State Council: "There is no doubt that serfdom, as it exists at present in our land, is an evil, palpable and obvious to all. But to touch it *now* would be a still more disastrous evil . . . . The Pugachev rebellion proved how far popular rage can go."[40] In fact, throughout his reign the emperor feared, at the same time, two different revolutions. There was the danger that the gentry might bid to obtain a constitution if the government decided to deprive the landlords of their serfs. On the other hand, an elemental popular uprising might also be unleashed by such a major shock to the established order as the coveted emancipation.

In the end, although the government was almost constantly concerned with serfdom, it achieved very little. New laws either left the change in the serfs' status to the discretion of their landlords, thus merely continuing Alexander I's well-meaning but ineffectual efforts, or they prohibited only certain extreme abuses connected with serfdom such as selling members of a single family to different buyers. Even the minor concessions granted to the peasants were sometimes nullified. For instance, in 1847, the government permitted serfs to purchase their freedom if their master's estate was sold for debt. In the next few years, however, the permission was made inoperative without being formally rescinded. Following the European revolutions of 1848, the meager and hesitant government solicitude for the serfs came to an end. Only the bonded peasants of Western Russian provinces obtained substantial advantages in the reign of Nicholas I. They received this preferential treatment because the government wanted to use them in its struggle against the Polish influence which was prevalent among the land-lords of that area.

Determined to preserve autocracy, afraid to abolish serf-dom, and suspicious of all independent initiative and popular participation, the emperor and his government could not intro-duce fundamental reforms. Important developments did never-theless take place in certain areas where change would not threaten the fundamental political, social and economic struct-ure of the Russian empire. Especially significant proved to be the codification of law and the far-reaching reform in the con-dition of the state peasants. The new code, produced in the late eighteen-twenties and the early eighteen-thirties by the im-mense labor of Speranskii and his associates, marked, despite defects, a tremendous achievement and a milestone in Russian jurisprudence. In January 1835 it replaced the ancient *Ulozhen-ie* of Tsar Alexis, dating from 1649, and it was destined to last until 1917. The reorganization of the state peasants followed several years later after Count Paul Kiselev became head of the new Ministry of State Domains in 1837. Kiselev's reform, which included the shift of taxation from persons to land, additional allotments for poor peasants, some peasant self-government, and the development of financial assistance, schools, and medical care in the villages, has received almost universal praise from prerevo-lutionary historians. The leading Soviet specialist on the subject, Professor N.M. Druzhinin, however, claimed recently, on the basis of impressive evidence, that the positive aspects of Kiselev's reform had a narrow scope and application, while fundamentally it placed an extremely heavy burden on the state peasants, made all the more difficult to bear by the exactions and malpractices of local administration.[41] Finance minister Kankrin's policy, and in particular his measures to stabilize the currency — often cited among the progressive developments in Nicholas I's reign — proved to be less effective and important in the long run than Speranskii's and Kiselev's work.

But even limited reforms became impossible after 1848. Frightened by European revolutions, Nicholas I became utterly reactionary. Russians were forbidden to travel abroad, an order which hit teachers and students especially hard. The number of students without government scholarships was limited to three hundred per university, except for the school of medicine. Uvarov had to resign as minister of education in favor of an entirely reactionary and subservient functionary, Prince Plato Shirinskii-Shikhmatov, who on one occasion told an assistant of his: "You should know that I have neither a mind nor a will of my own — I am merely a tool of the emperor's will."[42] New restrictions further curtailed university autonomy and academic freedom. Constitutional law and philosophy were eliminated from the curricula; logic and psychology were retained, but were to be taught by professors of theology. In fact, in the opinion of some historians, the universities themselves came close to being eliminated, and only the timely intervention of certain high officials prevented this disaster. Censorship reached ridiculous proportions, with new agencies appearing, including the dreaded "censorship over the censors," the so-called Buturlin committee. The censors, to cite only a few instances of their activities, deleted "forces of nature" from a textbook in physics, probed the hidden meaning of an ellipsis in an arithmetic book, changed "were killed" to "perished" in an account of Roman emperors, demanded that the author of a fortune-telling manual explain why in his opinion stars influence the fate of men, and worried about the possible concealment of secret codes in musical notations.[43] Literature and thought were virtually stifled. Even Pogodin was impelled in the very last years of the reign to accuse the government of imposing upon Russia "the quiet of a graveyard, rotting and stinking, both physically and morally."[44] It was in this atmosphere of suffocation that Russia experienced its shattering defeat in the Crimean War.

Official Nationality not only dominated Russia for thirty years, but also found application in foreign policy, a point incidentally which Presniakov, on the whole, failed to appreciate. Indeed, it had emerged as part of the reaction of established European regimes against the French Revolution and Napoleon and was thus international from the beginning. Nicholas I was determined to maintain and defend the existing order in Europe, just as he considered it his sacred duty to preserve the archaic system in his own country. He saw the two closely related as the whole and its part, and he thought both to be threatened by the same enemy: the many-headed hydra of revolution, which had suffered a major blow with the final defeat of Napoleon but refused to die. In fact, it rose again and again, in 1830, in 1848, and on other occasions, attempting to reverse and undo the settlement of 1815. True to his principles, the resolute tsar set out to engage the enemy. In the course of the struggle, the crowned "policeman of Russia" became also the "gendarme of Europe."

Although not to the exclusion of other considerations, this determined championing of legitimism — that international variant of autocracy — and established order explains much in Nicholas I's foreign policy in regard to such crucial developments as the Münchengrätz and Berlin agreements with Prussia and Austria, Russian policy towards the revolutions of 1830 and 1848, including large-scale military intervention in Hungary in 1849, and the Russian emperor's persistent hostility to such products of revolutions as Louis-Philippe's monarchy in France and the new state of Belgium. The great Polish uprising of 1830-18-31 only helped to underline to the monarch the direct connection between European revolution and revolt in his own domains, and, long after the military victory, the suppression of Polish danger remained his constant concern. From Don Carlos in Spain to Ernest Augustus in Hanover, Nicholas I was ready to support, or at least sympathize with, all manifestations of European reaction.

Yet, even for Nicholas I not every issue could be entirely clear. Unusually complex and difficult in his reign was the so-called Eastern Question which led to a war between Russia and Persia in 1826-1828, to the battle of Navarino in 1827 and a war between Russia and Turkey in 1828-1829, in connection with the Greek struggle for independence, to such striking diplomatic developments as the Treaty of Unkiar Skelessi of 1833, the Treaty of London of 1840, and the Straits Convention of 1841, and which finally exploded in the Crimean War. Still, although the last word on the Russo-Turkish relations in the first half of the nineteenth century has not been said, it would seem rash to dissociate Nicholas I's policy in the Near East from his general orientation. The Treaty of Adrianople of 1829 represented a moderate settlement which might have saved the Ottoman empire from destruction. The Treaty of Unkiar Skelessi, whatever its exact nature and implications, resulted from Nicholas I's quick response to the sultan in his hour of need against Mohammed Ali of Egypt, another revolutionary rebel in the eyes of the tsar. Even the Russian monarch's eventual interest in partitioning the Turkish empire can be construed as a product of the conviction that the Porte could not survive in the modern world, and that therefore the leading European states had to arrange for a proper redistribution of possessions and power in the Balkans and the Near East in order to avoid popular self-determination, anarchy, revolution, and war. In other words, Nicholas I's approach to Great Britain can be considered sincere, and the ensuing misunderstanding all the more tragic. However, one other factor must also be weighed in an appreciation of Nicholas I's Near Eastern policy: Orthodoxy. The Crimean War was provoked partly by religious conflicts. Moreover, the tsar himself retained throughout his reign a certain ambivalence toward the sultan. He repeatedly granted the legitimacy of the sultan's rule in the Ottoman Empire, but remained, nevertheless, uneasy about the sprawling Moslem state which believed in the Koran and oppressed its numerous Orthodox subjects. To resolve the difficulty, on one occasion Nicholas I actually proposed to the Turkish representative that the sultan become Orthodox![45] Once the hostilities began, the Russian emperor readily proclaimed himself the champion of the Cross against the infidels.

To repeat, the reign of Nicholas I resembled in many important and less important ways that of his older brother and predecessor. Neither sovereign challenged the fundamental

Russian realities of autocracy and serfdom. Both, however, enacted certain more modest and limited reforms. Nicholas I's
reorganization of state peasants can be considered as a more
substantial contribution to the kind of partial improvement in
peasant life inaugurated by such measures of Alexander I as the
law concerning the free agriculturists. Similarly, Speranskii's
codification of Russian law represented a logical continuation
of the work of that same Speranskii and others who tried to
improve the structure and functioning of the Russian government in the earlier reign. In foreign policy the younger brother was only too conscious of continuity with the older, of the
legacy of the Congress of Vienna and the alliance system. In
terms of principles, Nicholas I maintained the Russian tradition
of the emperor as both the all-powerful head and the first servant of the state, and he admired Peter the Great even more
fervently than had his predecessors. Even as to character, it is
worth remembering that Alexander I too was a perfectionist
and a drill sergeant, suspicious, given to rages, and determined
to keep all authority to himself in matters great and small. Both
militarism and obscurantism existed in Russia before 1825 as
well as after.

But the difference was also important. It was as if Nicholas I's rule reproduced and developed comprehensively many
basic aspects of his brother's rule. Alexander's reign, however,
like the emperor's baffling and contradictory character, had the
other side, which Nicholas's regime and Nicholas conspicuously
lacked. Alexander I was an autocrat, but an autocrat in love
with constitutions. He was a despot, but a despot who believed
in Enlightenment. Even his foreign policy could not be simply
summarized as legitimism and a defense of the *status quo*.
Whereas Alexander I talked about his determination to introduce Novosiltsev's constitution in Russia, a project that was for
him "sacred," Nicholas I, after the recapture of Warsaw, wrote
as follows to Prince Ivan Paskevich, the Russian commander,
concerning that same constitution which the Poles had found
and published:

NICHOLAS I AND THE COURSE OF RUSSIAN HISTORY

> Chertkov brought me a copy of the constitutional project for Russia found in Novosiltsev's papers. The publication of this paper is most annoying. Out of a hundred of our young officers ninety will read it, will fail to understand it or will scorn it, but ten will retain it in their memory, will discuss it — and, the most important point, *will not forget it.* This worries me above everything else. This is why I wish so much that the guards be kept in Warsaw as briefly as possible. Order Count Witt to try to obtain as many copies of this booklet as he can and to destroy them, also to find the manuscript and send it to me.[46]

Novosiltsev, to be sure, remained as a senior statesman of the empire. Indeed the efforts and aspirations of such figures as Nicholas Novosiltsev, Victor Kochubei, and Michael Speranskii himself, under Alexander I and under Nicholas I, illustrate admirable continuity, but also change, as regards the two reigns.

By foreclosing one main line of development Nicholas I transformed enlightened despotism into despotism pure and simple. Instead of reason and progress Russians were to rally around Orthodoxy, autocracy, and nationality. Instead of winning a future, they were to defend a past. Was it really worth defending? The answer extended beyond the reign of Nicholas I, and beyond Presniakov's perceptive little volume.

Nicholas V. Riasanovsky

INTRODUCTION

Nearly a half-century after its original publication, *Apogei samo-derzhaviia: Nikolai I* [*The Apogee of Autocracy: Nicholas I*] stands not only as a provocative evaluation of one of the most misunderstood rulers in modern Russian history, but as a monument to the analytical skill of its author, A.E. Presniakov. Born in 1878, Presniakov reached maturity in the stimulating years of the late nineteenth century, began his historical career during Russia's famed "Silver Age," experienced the Bolshevik Revolution as a mature and respected scholar, and – though himself a "bourgeois" historian – remained an eminent academician until his death in 1929. Despite his prominence and the durability of his historical works, relatively little is known about Presniakov as a person. His father served as an engineer in Tiflis (Tbilisi), and it was in this Caucasian city that Presniakov received his secondary education. He subsequently enrolled in the historical-philological faculty of St. Petersburg University (the present-day Leningrad University), one of the most distinguished institutions in Imperial Russia and the one with which Presniakov was destined to be associated, in a variety of capacities, throughout his life. It was at St. Petersburg that Presniakov studied under the outstanding Russian historian, S.F. Platonov. Like many students, the young Presniakov found it necessary to work while pursuing his advanced degrees, and he embarked upon a teaching career which ultimately provided him with valuable experience on all educational levels and with a life-long interest in the development of mass education. In 1907 he was appointed *Privat-dotsent* at St. Petersburg University, a position corresponding to that of a lecturer or instructor at a modern American university and which afforded him a small income. In 1918 he became a Professor at the same institution, and from 1919 also served as Professor (and later Dean) of the Archaeological Institute, as well as Director of the Institute of History of the Russian Association of Scientific Institutions for Research in the Social Sciences in Leningrad.

Presniakov's greatest fame rests upon his works dealing with early Russian history. His master's thesis on the authority of the prince in ancient Russia was expanded and published in 1909 under the title *Kniazhnoe pravo v drevnei Rusi* [*Princely Law in Ancient Rus'*]. In it, Presniakov examined the social structure of the period and launched the investigation of the development of Russian feudalism, a topic which subsequently became popular with other Russian historians. His research and writing already revealed the strong influence of the so-called "juridical school," led by B.N. Chicherin, K.D. Kavelin, and V. I. Sergeevich. These historians viewed the State as the essential idea behind the entire historical development of the nation and concentrated their attention upon institutional and legal history, especially in the ancient and medieval periods. Presniakov's doctoral dissertation, the work for which he is most noted, was similarly characterized by an emphasis upon the "needs of the state." Expanded and published in 1918, *Obrazovanie velikorusskago gosudarstva* [*The Formation of the Great Russian State*], a translation of which into English was published in 1970, was significant not only for its grounding in medieval Russian sources but for the originality of its interpretation. Whereas earlier historians had regarded the rise of Moscow and the consolidation and strengthening of the Russian state by the Muscovite rulers as being the result of a combination of greed, economic changes, or historical "accident," Presniakov advanced the idea that it was the result of a conscious "national" aspiration, a recognition of the necessity to form a consolidated state.

Following the Bolshevik Revolution of 1917, Presniakov continued his historical activity as professor, researcher, writer, and administrator. Although not an advocate of the Revolution, he was not its adversary either, but regarded it as an organic product of Russia's historical development. He had, indeed, begun to display an interest in modern Russian history more than a decade before the Revolution. In 1905 he had published a brief sketch on the Decembrists, which was later expanded into his highly-regarded *14 Dekabria 1825 goda* [*14 December 1825* (Leningrad, 1926)], and in 1906 he produced a study of the revolutionary movement of the third quarter of the nineteenth century, "Nakanune narodnichestva" ["On the Eve of Populism"]. Although Presniakov remained a "bourgeois-liberal" historian and was unable, in the words of the *Great Soviet Encyclopedia*, to "emancipate himself from bourgeois-idealistic methodology" in his researches, he nonetheless was able to accept and be accepted by the Soviet regime to a degree which permitted him to produce several short studies dealing with the widening gap between the autocracy and the masses in the nineteenth century. A brief essay on the autocracy of Alexander II appeared in 1923 ["Samoderzhavie Aleksandra II," *Russkoe Proshloe* (1923), Nos. 4, 4-5, 9], followed by a volume on Alexander I in 1924 and the present study of Nicholas I in 1925. Like the study of Alexander I, the latter volume is not a "history" of the reign of Nicholas I, but an analysis of it, an interpretive essay which deals selectively with key features of the ruler's personality, purposes, programs, and policies. One other major publication bears Presniakov's name: in 1938-39 his lecture notes from the pre-Revolutionary period (based upon a wide array of sources) were published posthumously as the two-volume *Lektsii po russkoi istorii* [*Lectures on Russian History*].

Presniakov's death, in 1929, cut short his planned synthesis of his ideas concerning the collapse of the autocracy. The major outlines of his interpretation can be deduced, however, from his analysis of the reign of Nicholas I. Whereas Nicholas traditionally had been viewed as a strong ruler heading a powerful state, Presniakov revealed his autocracy to be plagued by personal weakness and political impotence. The "beautiful autocracy" is shown to have been but a dream, and the dreamer Nicholas to have been helpless and frustrated in his efforts to solve the dilemmas of power in an age when social and

political discontent were on the rise, though often hidden behind the facade of stability. It is to Presniakov's credit that he
was able to deal with Nicholas as a man, not merely as a ruler,
and to indicate something of the personal as well as political
malaise which resulted from his camouflaged weakness.

At first glance it might appear that Presniakov's later works,
such as this volume on Nicholas I, have little connection with
his earlier, better-known works on princely law or the establishment of a unified Russian state. Yet, in fact, there is a strong
connection between them, for they deal with different phases
of a single historical process. In essence, Presniakov's earlier
works were focused upon the increase in monarchical power,
the unification of the nation, and the strengthening of the state
against foreign and domestic enemies. The later studies concen-
trate upon the dissipation of that power, the centripetal forces
of national and social heterogeneity, and the contradictions
within the state itself.

It is my hope that this translation of Presniakov's study of
Nicholas I will provide students of Russian and of modern European history not only with a brief analysis of the Nicholaevan
autocracy, but with the evidence also of the personal complexity of historical figures. Nicholas I has been stereotyped as "the
policeman of Russia and the gendarme of Europe." While the
validity of this image of Nicholas is undeniable, it conveys only
a partial understanding of the man — pious, stern, sentimental,
arrogant, and sometimes humble — whose reign with some irony
has been called the apogee of absolutism.

Judith C. Zacek

EMPEROR NICHOLAS I
THE APOGEE OF AUTOCRACY

CHAPTER I

MILITARY DYNASTIC DICTATORSHIP

The age of Nicholas I was an epoch of extreme reaffirmation of Russian autocratic power at the very moment when, in all the states of Western Europe, monarchical absolutism, stunned by a series of revolutionary shocks, was undergoing its final crises. In the West, the political system adopted new constitutional forms, while Russia was experiencing the flowering of autocracy in its most extreme practical and ideological manifestations. At the head of the Russian state stood the monolithic figure of Nicholas I — monolithic in his world-view, in his steadfast, consistent behavior. There were no complexities in this world-view, no oscillations in his straightforward conduct. Everything was reduced to some fundamental principle concerning power and the state, their purposes and problems. Such notions appeared as simple and as clear as the paragraphs of a military decree, and were bound together by the concept of duty, in the sense of military discipline, as the fulfillment of incurred obligations.

Throughout his entire life, not only in official declarations at the beginning of his reign but still later, even in his personal correspondence, Nicholas frequently repeated that imperial power had been thrust upon him unexpectedly, as though he had not known in advance how the question of succession to the throne had been resolved by his older brothers.[1] One has the impression that, by its frequent repetition, he almost convinced himself of the truth of this legend which he had personally placed in circulation, even though it did not correspond to reality. He wanted to believe it was true in essence: it well expressed his attitude toward power as a "trust" bestowed upon him by fate, a trust which he must preserve, cherish, strengthen and transfer intact to his successor. Quite unlike Catherine II, who searched for theoretical justifications for this power, or his brother Alexander I, who sought to harmonize it with contemporary political ideas and necessities, Nicholas held it to be a self-sufficient value which required neither justification nor explanation. Autocracy was, for him, an unshakable dogma. Nicholas perceived this venerable legacy, however, in a cultural-historical wrapping and on an ideological foundation corresponding to that of old Muscovite Russia, the medieval birthplace of that political order. The tradition of autocracy, in which Nicholas was reared, was most vividly characterized by two features which manifested themselves anew in Russian governing circles at the end of the eighteenth century: the strengthening of its dynastic base and the development of its militaristic pattern.

The Russian imperial dynasty took shape only in the time of Paul I (1796-1801). This dynasty was called Holstein-Gottorp in Germany, but in Russia it called itself "the House of Romanov," more because of national and political ties than blood relationships with the old ruling family, just as had the Austrian Habsburgs, who also descended from their "ancestors" only in the female line. The dynastic right of the "reigning house," which was barely contemplated in the days of the first Romanovs, could not have been established in the eighteenth century, when the sovereign authority found itself completely subordinated to the ruling noble class and the throne was controlled by the upper stratum of this class with the assistance of the military guards. Toward the end of the eighteenth century, the position of Russia in Europe's international revolution was defined and firmly established. Domestically, the contradictions in her economic system and social structure were intensified and the need to liberate the productive forces of the country from the burdensome ways of the "old order" became pressing. And the terrible shocks of the *Pugachevshch-ina*[2] generated in the ruling class an eagerness to strengthen the central authority so as to bolster the existing "order" and hold back the frightening flood of social conflict. Both of these contradictory tendencies created favorable conditions for the reaffirmation of the sovereign as the ruler of the destiny of the country.

On the eve of the nineteenth century, this sovereign authority was reorganized by means of administrative reforms which strengthened the central government and by "fundamental" legislation, the goal of which was the affirmation of the political and legal status of the monarchy and dynasty. This question was settled by Paul in his statutes of 1797.[3] By the "General Statement" on succession to the throne and by the "Statute of the Imperial House," he created a new dynastic law. For this reason, both of these statements were proclaimed as "the fundamental laws of the empire."

The successor to a series of fortuitous figures on the imperial throne, and himself the father of a large family (four sons and five daughters), Paul felt himself to be the real founder of the dynasty. "The increase of the family," by which the proper inheritance of the throne would be assured, he smugly listed in first place among the "firm foundations" of every monarchy, and — along with "the affirmation of the continuous right of succession to the throne" — he considered it necessary, as "head of the family," to determine the position of the entire "family" in the state and its internal routine. In the legislation of Paul I, modeled upon the House Statute (*Hausgesetze*) of the German ruling families, the imperial dynasty for the first time received definition. Its entire membership, both male and female, in all its lines and branches was amalgamated in terms of possible succession to the throne and examined in minute detail, no longer from the point of view of the "house" but of the "fundamental" law of the empire. The entire "family" was sharply distinguished from civil society. The "imperial family," the "ruling house" henceforth became a special organization, all members of which

occupied an utterly exclusive position outside the normal bounds
of both public and civil law. The isolation of the dynasty was
increased further by the supplemental action of Alexander I in
1820, on the occasion of the marriage of his brother Constantine to Countess Joanna Grudzinska (Princess Lowicz).[4] The
dynasty could maintain itself only through marriages of its
members to persons who also belonged to some ruling family.
This particular marriage, on the contrary, although legal in civil
terms was illegal in political terms. That is, it did not confer
upon the person whom a member of the imperial family married, nor upon their children, any dynastic rights or privileges.

These legislative decisions were reflected in numerous
everyday occurrences. The "family" lived its own separate life,
in the narrow and secluded *milieu* of the court and ruling circles, alienated and isolated by numerous conventions from Russian social life and in general from Russian reality. The internal life, attitudes, and traditions of this family, semi-Russian not
only in its origins but in its marital ties, took on a special character. The court of Nicholas's parents was generally under
strong German influence, thanks to the Württemberg relationship of the Empress and the Holstein legacy and Prussian sympathies of Paul.

The significance of "Prussian friendship" throughout the
life and activity of Alexander I (1801-1825) is well known. The
familial feelings and ties of the tsar's family embraced not only
its Russian members but also numerous Prussian, Württemberg,
Mecklenburg, Saxe-Weimar, Baden, and many other kinsmen,
ties with whom augmented the general European significance
of Russian imperial power and enmeshed Russia in international politics. The familial and proprietary concepts of the German princely houses had a strong influence upon Russian dynastic views. Nicholas I grew up in this atmosphere and it was
as his own. These ties became still deeper and stronger with
his marriage in 1817 to the daughter of Frederick William III
of Prussia, Charlotte (known in Russia as Alexandra Fedorovna).
His father-in-law was like a father to him. Having been born in

1796, he really did not know his own father. His feelings toward his brother, Alexander I, who was eighteen years his senior, were more filial than fraternal, but the two were never close. The education of the younger sons of Paul had been entrusted entirely to their mother, Maria Fedorovna.[5] Nicholas reverently adhered to Alexander's political legacies of the period of the Holy Alliance, but without those mystical and cosmopolitan undertones and pseudo-liberal utopian ideas with which Alexander complicated them. Nicholas adopted only those precepts in which Alexander resembled Frederick William III, whose memory he revered throughout his life and to whom he referred in letters to Frederick William III's son and successor, the Empress's favorite brother, Frederick William IV, not as father-in-law but as father. Prussian patriarchal monarchy together with formal military discipline and religious-moral principles, in the sense of an obligation of service and loyalty to the traditional order, appealed to him as the foundation of those "principles of authority" which it was necessary (so he dreamed) to re-establish in a Europe which had forgotten them. It was these he meant when he referred to the legacies of his dear "father" Frederick and his brother Alexander, of which he alone was the true guardian. In Russian court circles and in St. Petersburg "higher" society in general, the German element from this time became ever stronger. The role of Lieven and Adlerberg[6] stemmed from the fact that the primary education of the younger children of Paul I had been entrusted to their forebearers (who were members of the "Russian" aristocracy). The *milieu* of the Baltic German nobility, with its aristocratic and monarchistic traditions, was especially close to the tsar's family during the anxious period of unrest throughout the European political world. "The Russian nobility serves the state, the [Baltic] German nobility serves us," Nicholas later declared, disclosing with utter frankness the special nature of his gratitude to the Baltic Germans. The Courlander Lamsdorff,[7] the former director of the cadet corps, was the mentor of the younger sons of Paul when they were growing up; the

stiff, harsh methods of this cadet-corps pedagogue fostered in
Nicholas certain habits for which there was yet another powerful source in his military education.

Toward the beginning of the nineteenth century, monarchical power took on a militaristic character everywhere but in
England. It was especially strong and clear in Prussia and in
Russia. Prussian militarism was established in the life of the
Russian army under Peter III and anew, and in its most extreme
forms, under Paul. In the court and governmental circles the
grandees of the eighteenth century were replaced by men in
dress uniform and with military bearing; in court life the par-
ade-ground style became still more deeply rooted; the principles of military command and martial discipline permeated all
aspects of government. Imperious authority and silent obedience, sharp commands and stern rebukes, disciplinary penal-
ties and cruel punishments − such were the fundamental methods of administration, alternating with a system of rewards
for distinction, which encouraged displays of the "supreme"
good will and favor. Service and loyalty "to one's sovereign"
embodied the fulfillment of civic duty and replaced it, along
with the suppression of all independent public activity. The
"Gatchina discipline,"[8] created by Paul and developed by
Arakcheev,[9] gave rise to a tradition not unlike that of an army
command.

The school of martial bearing elaborated and defined itself in many ways in the character and views of Nicholas. It is
known that the Empress-Mother attempted to limit the military passions of her sons. But she did not and could not succeed in this attempt. The militaristic roots were too deeply
implanted. In the trivial details of the parade-watch, which
were agonizing for the troops, Alexander found respite from
the fine points of his politics and from the complexity of his
hopeless political experiments. Nicholas became an artist of
martial articulation, although in this he yielded the palm to his
brother Michael. Schooled in the most complex, artificial ways,
disciplined in the regularity of large-scale movements,

mechanically obedient to command, the army provided a series of brilliant pictorial impressions, which Nicholas recalled with genuine delight in letters to his wife. "The sovereign's relaxation with his troops is his only real pleasure," wrote his associate Benckendorff,[10] on his own admission. No other experience gave him such complete satisfaction, such sure confidence in his own power and in the triumph of "order" over the complex contradictions and turbulent arbitrariness of human life and nature.

"The militarism for which you were reproached was merely your appreciation of politics," wrote a Decembrist[11] to Nicholas from prison. The word "merely" here is a reflection of the circumstances in which the letter was written, but politics were involved in Nicholas's militarism just as much as militarism was involved in his politics. Both elements of his outlook and activity were entwined, growing together organically. The army, a powerful and obedient force in the hands of the emperor, was the government's most important fulcrum of strength and, at the same time, the best school for the loyal execution of the imperial will. Inspections and parades, martial ceremonies into which Nicholas threw himself with such enthusiasm, were not only a "real pleasure" but also an impressive demonstration of this strength to those at home and abroad and, perhaps most of all, to himself.

Nicholas not only pursued battlefront service with enthusiasm and success, but also received a solid military education in general. From his scholarly and gifted teachers and from his own lively interest he gained a basic familiarity with military engineering and with strategical methods. The latter he studied practically, in particular by analyzing the most important military campaigns of the war of 1814-15, and by studying strategical problems, for example the plan for a war against the unified forces of Prussia and Poland or against Turkey to drive the Turks from Europe. During the wars which occurred in his own reign, he personally guided the establishment of plans of military operations and often peremptorily imposed his own

directives upon his generals. And construction matters, not only
of a military nature, remained one of his favorite enterprises. He
spent considerable time inspecting building projects, making
changes in them, personally approving them, and following their
progress to completion. On the other hand, he was bored by
judicial affairs and political science. His teachers, although outstanding in the profundity of their thought and knowledge, were
poor pedagogues – Balugiansky and Storch[12] – who only succeeded in strengthening that aversion to "abstract ideas" which
characterized his nature and mental processes. An understanding of "law" remained alien to Nicholas's world-view. To him,
juridical norms were only laws, like the commands of the sovereign, and obedience to them was based upon the loyalty of
subjects who were brought up to display pious humility before
higher authority. "The best theory of law," he said, "is good
morality, and it must be at heart independent of abstract notions and have religion as its foundation." Better than the theories of "natural law" which were taught to him by Professor
Kukolnik[13] were the reactionary, romantic ideas of German political literature, which were so esteemed in his beloved Berlin.

These views were reflected in the original doctrine expounded by Ya. I. Rostovtsev[14] in 1848 in the "Precepts for the Enlightenment of Students of Military Educational Institutions."
Here the power of the state was endowed with the significance
of higher authority in all social relations. The supreme power
is the "social conscience," and it must have the same meaning
for the activity of a man that individual conscience has for his
inner motives. "The law of conscience, the moral law, is binding on him as a guide for his personal will; the law of supreme
power, the positive law, is binding on him as a guide for his social relations." The will of men, who compose society, is, according to this theory, an anarchistic element, since "in society
the conflict of diverse wills is inevitable," and therefore, "in
order to preserve society from destruction and to strengthen
the moral order within it," the hegemony of some other force –
a supreme power – is essential. It creates the basis of a "social

conscience" through its statutes, the purpose of which is to suppress the conflict of diverse aspirations and interests, individuals and social groups, in the name of an "order" which is denoted as "moral." A firm support for this "law of supreme authority" must be provided by the ecclesiastical-religious education of youth to render "unlimited devotion" to the will of the Heavenly Father, and "submission to temporal authority, which is divinely given." Nicholas's political conservatism was accompanied by his own, quite undiluted psychological and pedagogical theory. In it was found the moral support of the omnipotence of the government, as the source of social order, morality, and culture: outside the governmental order there was only the chaos of individual personalities.

This simplistic philosophy of life, which was characteristic of the period, was also Nicholas's own personal world-view. "Here," he said, explaining the motives underlying his admiration for the Prussian army, "there is order, strict, unconditional legality, no claims to know everything and no contradictions, all things flow one from the other. No one gives orders until he himself has learned how to obey; no one stands before another without a lawful basis. All are subordinated to a single defined purpose, all have their assignments. That is why I feel so well among these people and why I will always hold in respect the profession of soldier. I look upon all human life in the same way as I look upon service, for each person serves."

CHAPTER II

BUREAUCRATIC NATIONALISM

The reign of Nicholas I was the golden age of Russian nationalism. Russia and Europe consciously confronted each other as two different cultural and historical worlds, fundamentally different in their political, religious, national life and character. During the reign of Alexander I it had appeared that the process of the "Europeanization" of Russia was reaching its limits. The elaboration of projects of political reform of the empire seemed to have prepared the Russian political order for a transition to the European form of a bourgeois state. The epoch of congresses had made Russia an organic part of the "European concert" of international alliances and had brought her foreign policy within the bounds of the general European political system. The constitutional Kingdom of Poland was established, according to the purpose of the Russian ruler, as a model for the general rebuilding of the empire, and was intended not so much as an outpost which delimited Russia from Europe but as a wide bridge to connect them. Even in economic relations, the agreement of the powers on measures to facilitate trade between the parts of the truncated Polish territory was given a broadened interpretation and led, in 1817, to such a break in the system of prohibitive protective tariffs that it generated deep anxiety for the fate of infant Russian industry. Finally, the church and administrative, and the religious and educational policies in the spirit of the general European reaction during the era of the Holy Alliance led to a unique levelling of the "distinctive" characteristics of Russian life even in this area.

The vigorous reaction against all of these tendencies of the Alexandrine epoch united the disparate interests and tendencies of Russian society. All of Alexander I's policies, both domestic and foreign, encountered sharp and angry criticism, incessant opposition, which reflected the interests and needs of various social groups but were united in one respect, by a national and patriotic sentiment which was hostile to the "Emperor of Europe," as they called him. The voice of the conservative elements in this opposition sounded ever louder in Karamzin's *Memoir on Ancient and Modern Russia*.[1] Karamzin was equally hostile to constitutional experiments and ministerial, bureaucratic administration; he championed instead the old Russian autocracy. "We are not England; for so many centuries we have seen our fate in the monarch and have acknowledged his benign will as the highest authority . . . . In Russia the sovereign is the living law: he shows mercy to the good and punishes the wicked, and the love of the former overcomes the fear of the latter . . . . In the Russian monarch all power is unified; our government is paternal and patriarchal." "Autocracy is the palladium of Russia." Ministers, insofar as they are required, "must be merely secretaries to the sovereign on various matters." The emperor must find support for his authority not in the bureaucracy, but in the nobility, which is hereditary and permanent and not ephemeral and mobile, advancing by promotion in the ranks. The responsibility for administration must be in the hands of this nobility. The nobility and the clergy, the Senate and the Holy Synod, as guardians of tradition, and above them the Sovereign-Lawgiver, the source of all authority: "that is the basis of the Russian monarchy." Karamzin's ideal was the aristocratic monarchy of the eighteenth century; to him it was a national object of veneration. Autocratic power is a protective force for the aristocratic state. The sovereign must be the head of the nobility; in them alone

must he find the support of his throne. The letter which
Alexander I received on concluding the Treaty of Tilsit[2]
(which the nobility despised) and which, apparently, must
also be attributed to Karamzin, expressed these same views
no less distinctly. Unity with the nobility alone can resolve the problems arising out of the early years of Alexander I's reign: unity of administration and the replace-
ment of arbitrariness by legality. "In that mutual trust between sovereign and nobility you will find the means to
give us a stable, integrated government whose members will
be animated by the same spirit and whose labors will be
directed toward a single goal." Reading here we find a cun-
ning approval of the sovereign who had begun his reign with
the idea of "subordinating himself to the salutary authority
of the laws," who had restored the violated rights of "the
first pillars of the throne" (the nobility and the guardian
of its rights, the Senate), and who had surrounded himself
with "statesmen proposed by a general movement," that is,
by the public opinion of the nobility itself. And thus, according to Karamzin, must the ruler act. If he wishes to
be patriotic and popular, let him banish "foreign influences"
and be inspired by "unlimited confidence in his own nation," let him rely only upon "true Russians." Only then
will the government become strong and attain the "unity
of purpose and that fortunate agreement on the details of
its fulfillment, without which even the greatest genius can
accomplish nothing to save the state."

These views expressed, primarily, the interests of the
highest stratum of the nobility, the aristocrats and magnates
who dreamed of having their social privileges and the political relationships of the Russian Empire of the eighteenth
century affirmed "permanently and inviolably." But Alexander I's policies evoked in other strata of the nobility
another type of opposition, which took shape in the latter
years of his reign and culminated in the Decembrist movement. This opposition was less unified, more complex in

motives and lines of thought, and became the cradle of a
series of social trends which were broadly dispersed in
their subsequent development. But in all the varied programs of this movement the common, fundamental characteristic was a striving for the renewal of Russian life, for
its reorganization on new principles of civil rights for the
masses and political influence for the middle classes of society, for a broad development of industry, trade, and education — in a word, for the bases of a Western European
bourgeois system. But another equally common characteristic was a nationalistic and patriotic attitude that opposed
the cosmopolitanism of Alexander's reign. This movement,
which can be called national and liberal, broke with the
traditions of the old feudal nobility and with the autocracy.

The movement developed chiefly within the lesser landed nobility and in the officer corps, where the most progressive elements of Russian society were concentrated in this
period. It espoused a seizure of power by means of a military coup, avoiding a mass revolutionary movement, and
it culminated in the dramatic episode of December 14,
1825, on Senate Square.

Both of these social trends of the Alexandrine epoch
had an extremely strong influence upon Nicholas I. He met
them face to face: the first in the decisive turn of governmental activity away from its former path in the last years
of Alexander's reign, the second in the dramatic circumstances of his accession to the throne.

During his brother's lifetime, Nicholas did not take an
active part in political life; he merely commanded a guard
division and administered the military engineering corps.
Nicholas well understood the military and court *milieu* in
which he moved, the so-called "higher" society, with all
its hollowness and dissoluteness, its squabbles and intrig-
ues. He later found that the time expended in the crowd-
ed antechambers of the nobility and in secretarial offices
had not been wasted: it served as "invaluable practice for

the understanding of people and personalities," and here he "saw much, understood much, and discovered much — and seldom erred." In the salons of this circle there developed what was then regarded in St. Petersburg as public opinion: it was the opinion of the higher nobility and bureaucracy, and Nicholas knew its value to him. He had no more sympathy and esteem for this society than Paul or Alexander I had had. He regarded the nobility first of all as a service class which he tried to discipline and maintain as a submissive tool of authority. In moments which were difficult for authority and dangerous to its bearer, the official acts and personal addresses of Nicholas sounded Karamzin-like, looking upon the nobility as the "bulwark of the throne," speaking of the government as the safeguard of its interests. He was able, on occasion, to call himself "the first noble" and to reckon himself as a "St. Petersburg landowner."

But he was too much the "commander" to maintain such a tone in his attitude toward the upper class. And the contradictions of Russian life in the era of the breakdown of serfdom and the growth of commercial and industrial interests were too sharp to permit Nicholas to maintain himself firmly as a "nobles' tsar." Noble society itself, having experienced a complicated internal crisis, did not give the government enough confidence in it as a conservative force, as a mainstay of the established order in the empire. Commanding guards units (a brigade, later a division), Nicholas was extremely dissatisfied by the "dissolute, utterly depraved" conduct and attitudes of the guards who had returned from the foreign campaigns. "Subordination had vanished," he wrote in his remarks concerning the events of December 14, "and was preserved only at the front; respect for officers disappeared completely, and service was a thing of the past, for there were neither rules nor order and everything was done arbitrarily and capriciously." Perhaps it was hindsight, but Nicholas noted that

he sensed that "something important was behind this," that
"insolent chatterers" who had destroyed discipline, that school
of political loyalty, "had formed a chain throughout the regi-
ments and had found protectors in society." Nicholas responded to such impressions with special drills, with that intensified
"militarism" in which Alexander Bestuzhev[3] had detected "the
appreciation of politics."

The impact of the Decembrist affair of 1825 upon Nicholas was all the stronger because the conspiracy and revolt had
originated in the military environment, which provided only a
concentrated expression of sentiments spread widely among
the masses. Investigation and punishment of the Decembrists
became the first official act of Emperor Nicholas I. He participated personally in all its details, playing the part of an adroit
interrogator and jailer who knew how to use both cruel intimi-
dation and feigned magnanimity to loosen the tongue. He directed the investigating commission in everything, acted as judge
through a figure-head "supreme criminal court," and pronounced the sentences prescribed by the court, having made certain
changes in them beforehand. December 14 was deeply etched
in his memory. From this day he reckoned his accession to the
throne, on its anniversary he celebrated the twenty-fifth anniversary of his reign, and he reminisced about it annually both
in conversations with his associates and in letters: "What an
anniversary!" Throughout his life he indeed remained the war-
den of the Decembrists: he followed their every movement in
distant exile; he received reports about the details of their existence; he personally, and often sternly, decided questions a-
bout the fate of the Decembrists themselves and their families.
His "Decembrist-friends" he called to mind at every disquieting
display of criticism and opposition.

Behind this acute impression of his first confrontation
with political activity there was concealed nothing more substantial than a simple nervous memory of the danger he had experienced and the anxiety he had endured. Nicholas carefully
listened and attentively read the testimony of the Decembrists,

and tried to grasp the system of thought and feelings which were so alien to him and to discern the contradictions and inadequacies of Russian life in the picture uncovered before him. The director of affairs of the investigating commission was entrusted with compiling a collection of opinions on various aspects of the conditions in the state which the Decembrists had expressed in their testimony and by which they had explained the general dissatisfaction which had summoned them to attempt a coup. The memorandum by this bureaucrat turned out to be an instructive summary of the many difficult problems the new government would have to resolve. "It is necessary to grant clear, positive laws; to foster justice by instituting the briefest possible legal proceedings; to elevate the moral education of the clergy; to support the nobility, despairing and utterly ruined by debts to credit institutions; to revive trade and industry by means of firm regulations; to direct the education of youth appropriate to the status of each individual; to improve the position of landowners; to eliminate the degrading sale of people; to revive the fleet; to encourage individuals to enter the field of navigation; and, in a word, to set right the innumerable disorders and abuses." The pen which had expounded the guilt of the "criminals" now composed, upon the command of the sovereign and in the words of the Decembrists, a sketch of the condition of a state which was so shattered by "innumerable disorders and abuses" that there remained no solution save a fundamental alteration of the entire governmental system and perhaps even of the foundations of the state.

The Decembrists themselves, in their letter testaments to Nicholas, transferred to him, as it were, their own unfinished business. According to Kochubei,[4] the Chairman of the State Council, a compendium of their comments and evaluations was constantly at Nicholas's hand and he often glanced at it and gave copies of it to Kochubei and to Crown Prince Constantine. His "Decembrist-friends" poisoned the autocrat's consciousness in two ways: by generating a cautious distrust of society, which had been ready to take up revolutionary methods against the authority that impeded the growth of Russian life; and by creating an understanding that the "general dissatisfaction" about which there was so much alarming gossip could not be attributed to ideological "delusions," but had an objective basis in the problems of Russian life, which had outgrown the constraints of its social and political order.

One of the foreign observers of St. Petersburg life at that time has noted, as a cauše of the peculiar alarm that the government felt, that the minds of "the most prudent people" were permeated by persistent thoughts concerning the necessity of reform, that it was dangerous to stand still and was essential, albeit with reasonable gradualness, "to go with the times" and prepare for "more decisive changes."

A brief but significant conclusion was drawn from all these complex impressions and expressed in the manifesto which Nicholas issued at the close of the judicial proceedings of the Decembrist case. The uprising had revealed "the secret of a long-standing evil," its suppression had "cleansed the fatherland of traces of the contagion which had been hidden within it for so many years." This "contagion" had come from the West, as something alien and superficial. "This design does not reside in either the Russian character or disposition," but all efforts at a speedy eradication of this evil would be in vain without the unanimous support of all of society. Nicholas called on all classes to be united in loyalty to the government, but he particularly reminded the nobility of its importance as the bulwark of the throne and as the class to which all the paths of military and civilian service were open. Especially the nobility had to lend support to the "stability of the existing order, the security and property of its guardians," and to disseminate "patriotic, natural, not foreign education." The need for reforms would be satisfied "not by impudent, always destructive daydreams," but by gradual improvements in the existing order through governmental measures. Society could assist in this by expressing, through legal means, "every modest desire for improvement, every idea for strengthening the force of law and for the spread of genuine enlightenment and industry" which could be adopted "with good will."

Thus all social classes must yield in full confidence before the imperial authority and cooperate as much as possible, not from fear alone but as a matter of conscience, in the realization of its national, conservative program. This program had taken precedence over other currents even in the latter years of Alexander's reign, when, on the one hand, liberal dreams were abandoned, and on the other, the nationalistic banner was raised in matters of foreign and domestic policy. Even Alexander I, in the last two or three years of his life and reign, broke with the projects for reforming the political structure of the empire, sharply altered his attitude toward Poland, repudiated the dependence of Russia's Near Eastern policy upon the doctrines of the Holy Alliance, returned to protective tariffs, and abandoned his ecumenical point of view in matters of religious administration and popular education in favor of an Orthodox ecclesiastical reaction. The precepts of Alexander's last years became the program of Nicholas's reign.

CHAPTER III

CONTRADICTIONS OF THE NICHOLAEVAN EPOCH

The thirty-year period when power resided in the hands of Nicholas I was an epoch of acute contradictions in Russian life. The old order of state and social relations which had been built up over the centuries still held sway exclusively, but the economic, civil, and spiritual life of the country struggled against the old restraints which bound her ever more tightly. This period was the golden age of great Russian literature, the epoch of the first blossoming of Russian social thought and of independent Russian science, Russian theater, and Russian art, at the very time of an extreme submergence of Russian public opinion and national life under conditions of serfdom and a harsh governmental regime. In the economy there was a decided increase in commercial and industrial enterprise, under the hegemony of obsolete and corrupting forms of serfdom. In international relations there was a significant growth in the participation of Russia in world trade and in her influence on general European political affairs, at the same time as there was an acute alienation of Russia from the Western European world, as something foreign, dangerous, and hostile. Nicholas came upon the historical scene at the turning-point when the entire European world was changing from "the old order" to new forms of organization of the material bases and socio-political relations of national life. The processes which brought about this great change were even more strongly pronounced in Russia than elsewhere and forced her to experience a deep internal crisis, which was all the more severe because here, more than anywhere else, the country was weighed down by the heavy burden of the traditional forms of her political and social order.

The general condition of the economy foreshadowed the downfall of serfdom. The profitability of manorial estates undoubtedly declined; their debts rapidly accumulated. The Committee of Ministers was flooded with petitions for the granting of special privileges and deferred payments on the loans taken out by nobles, and both local administrators and the Ministry of Finance helplessly lamented the sharp increase of arrears in payments from the serfs. Serfdom was becoming ever more unprofitable, and was actually decaying in the new conditions of economic life. But its stagnant forms persisted and hindered all attempts to find a solution in a more rational, intensive economy with broadened production and sale in both foreign and domestic markets, which would gradually be established in connection with the revitalization of industry. On most manorial estates, this crisis had led only to an increase in *obrok* and a reinforcement of *barshchina*,[1] indeed to an even heavier pressure of serfdom upon the peasantry. Along with this, the bitterness of the serf population increased. The struggle against the mass flight of privately-owned serfs to the frontier regions still being colonized led to the placement of military cordons along their routes. Cases of peasant unrest and revolts became more frequent, and toward the end of the Nicholaevan epoch they increasingly assumed the character of a mass movement and their manifestations became more frightening, being accompanied by the murder of landowners and their stewards, arson, and acts of violence. The very foundation of the old system of serfdom was being shattered. Even the landed nobility was degenerating. Noble estates diminished and were fragmented. Among the provincial nobility there was a rapid growth of the small gentry and even of utterly landless nobles who neither by their economic security nor by their education nor by their style of life bore a resemblance to the "noble" and "ruling" class. Local assemblies of nobles suffered an acute diminution, and the more prosperous and enlightened elements among them poured into urban centers, shunning rural life and provincial activity. Districts administered by local assemblies of nobles since the time of Catherine II's provincial reform[2] were thoroughly neglected and abandoned. What were called "local needs" — the important work of caring for roads and the like, food supplies for the people, the struggle against epidemics, and so forth — remained virtually unmet, and the funds allocated for them mysteriously disappeared, unaccountably and unproductively.

Above the shaky and disturbed economic and cultural foundation of this local life rose the enormous edifice of the empire with its centralized institutions and formal, unlimited power. How was this power really exercised? Of a population of 52-53 million, according to the census of the 1830's, 25 million serfs were under the authority of their masters; as many as 18 million peasants on state and crown lands were under special administration, as property of the state and Imperial Family; and of the remaining nine million one must exclude the entire army, in order to get an approximate idea of what was actually governed by the general administrative institutions. The incredible insignificance and perversity of this administration was the natural result of its impotence and its miserable lack of influence in a *milieu* where 272,000 land and serf owners held dominion.

An accurate picture of the internal state of Russia is drawn with ample detail and clarity in the official documents of the reign of Nicholas I: in the records of the Committee of Ministers, in the executive reports of the Ministers of Internal Affairs and of Finance, and so on. Nicholas was acquainted with this reality, having been rather well prepared for it by the testimony of the Decembrists. It might be said that an ever broader and clearer picture of the pressing needs of the country and of the authority of the state was constantly being drawn before him. One of his first acts, upon the conclusion of the Decembrist case, was to order the so-called

Committee of December 6, 1826, to examine all the projects
of reform planned under Alexander I and to devise proposals
for urgent reforms, especially in the structure of state institutions and in the status of social classes. Then, throughout
his entire reign, a series of "committees" worked on financial, economic, judicial, and organizational problems which persistently and sharply presented themselves.

Whenever a serious difficulty confronted governmental
authority in running the country, it became clear once the
facts were examined that at the root of every vital question
concerning the means of extirpating disorder lay the fatal
problem of the old order, that of serfdom and Russian society. As the indissoluble link between all aspects of national
and state life and the principles of serfdom became clearer,
the necessity of a thorough renovation of the entire structure upon new foundations was advanced. The need for decisive action on the part of the government and the strengthening of state intervention in the established order and in the
very organization of local public life was clarified. With the
recognition of the powerlessness of available social groups to
overcome the opposition of conservative elements and to take
on the work of reorganizing the country, an active, revolutionary initiative was awaited from the essentially omnipo-
tent autocratic power. Even among the most "leftist" elements of the contemporary intelligentsia, there was a strong
awareness of this powerlessness and a reliance upon monarchical power in the matter of reform. Thus, for example, Belinsky, not in the period of his notorious enthusiasm for a "re-
conciliation with reality" but in 1847 and soon after his "revolutionary" letter to Gogol,[3] expressed confidence that the
"patriarchal, slumberous way of life is being overcome and
must follow another road," but the first step on this "other
road" — the emancipation of the peasants — was expected
through the "will of the Sovereign Emperor" who alone could
resolve the great problem, if only he did not place his trust
in the "friends of their own interests and enemies of the common good" who surrounded the throne.

But the "friends of their own interests" knew how to instill in their ruler an awareness of the connection between those interests and his own autocratic, dynastic ones. They impressed him both positively and negatively: on the one hand, with the idea that the authority of the landlord is a necessary support of autocratic power, and, on the other hand, that rushing into a reorganization of social relations inevitably would lead to revolutionary shocks. The liquidation of serfdom seemed fraught with great dangers to the autocracy. In governing circles, Karamzin's old idea was adopted, that "the nobility, scattered throughout the state, cooperated with the monarch in the preservation of tranquility and public order," and if the sovereign, "having divested them of this supervisory authority, would take all of Russia on his own shoulders," he would be unable to support such a weight. The theoretician of the Nicholaevan governmental system, Count S.S. Uvarov,[4] Minister of Public Instruction, affirmed that "the question of serfdom is closely linked to the question of autocracy and even one-man rule: these two are parallel forces which developed together, as a single historical principle, and they are equally legitimate." He spoke of serfdom: "This tree was deeply rooted long ago; it casts its shadow over both church and throne, and to uproot it is impossible." Nicholas officially expressed the view that the nobility was "the class to which, above all, is entrusted the protection of the throne and the fatherland," meaning, however, to acknowledge the basis of the nobility's privileged position as landowners, not as serfowners.

In the effort to separate these two questions Nicholas was definitely influenced by the situation in the Baltic provinces, where a so-called emancipation of the peasants had been introduced by Alexander I without an allotment to them of the nobles' lands and where administrative and judicial authority over them had been preserved by the landowners.[5] The latter did not actually correspond to Nicholas's autocratic convictions. The bureaucratization of local government

would have been more in keeping with his inclination. Certain
steps in this direction were taken in the reform of 1837:[6] the
districts were divided into sub-districts, with the appointment
of sub-district police officers and district assessors by the provincial administration. But this step was not followed up: both
the police officials and the assessors still were chosen primarily
from among the local landowners. As for the holding of land,
Nicholas declared that landed property was "permanently inviolable in the hands of the nobility," as a guarantee of "future
tranquillity." He tried, however, to prepare the way for a transition from serfdom to a "transitional status" in a proposal concerning "obligated" peasants, by which the landowner, preser-
ving his hereditary property rights, would grant his peasants
personal freedom and a specified piece of land in return for
duties and payments on the basis of a special inventory of each
estate. This measure, according to the project worked out by
Kiselev,[7] would be carried out throughout the state, independent of the will of individual landowners.

But these proposals encountered such angry and persistent opposition in the circles of the higher noble bureaucracy
that Nicholas hurriedly retreated. The draft of the new law was
introduced in the State Council in such altered form that it was
deprived of any serious importance, and the emperor, in his
speech to the Council and in the explanatory circular of the
Ministry of Internal Affairs, accompanied it with so many reservations that one foreign observer could well call the whole
affair a "tragicomedy." In this characteristic speech, Nicholas
said: "There is no doubt that serfdom, in its present form, is
an evil perceptible to all, but to tamper with it now would be
even more disastrous." "The present situation is such," he
went on, "that it cannot continue but, at the same time, dras-
tic measures to eliminate it are also impossible without a general upheaval." These hopeless words reveal the fundamental
attitude of Nicholas's government: the bitter fear of any sort
of "upheaval" paralyzed the recognition that the existing order "could not continue." And the law concerning obligated

peasants lost its force in the stipulation that its implementation depended upon the will of those landowners who themselves wished to do so, and in the explanation that it would eliminate the "harmful principle" of Alexander I's law concerning free cultivators — the alienation of a portion of land to the ownership of peasants — and would guarantee the preservation of the nobility's hereditary ownership of even those lands which were used by obligated peasants. In sum, this was merely a new victory for the nobility over the "prejudices" of the peasants, who felt that despite their personal enserfment they still were the actual owners of the land.

The nobility proved to be a force to be reckoned with and not just to be ordered about. A foreign observer found that Nicholas, although he retained enough respect from those about him to avoid the fate of Paul I, nonetheless took many chances, and the slightest false step on such slippery ground could ruin him. It was decidedly dangerous for the Russian sovereign to quarrel with the nobility, and this was so not only because it was hazardous to irritate the ruling class. The tractability of the autocracy in relation to the nobility, like the loyalty of the nobility to the throne, that is, their impulse to solidarity, was supported by their common fear of the danger of an angry outburst of the people. This fear compelled the ruling circles to ponder the necessity of relieving the tense atmosphere by means of reforms, but it also fostered indecision when they were attacked by fears that to touch the rickety edifice would bring about its total destruction. Nicholas's brother, Crown Prince Constantine, insisted on the inadmissability of "basic reforms which would alter the mutual relationships among classes," since this would lead inevitably to a change in the very foundations of the state system of the empire. And many people thought similarly at that time. They were convinced that the abolition of serfdom would lead to the abolition of autocracy. They felt that the establishment of a bourgeois social system upon the principles of civil liberties and private property would lead unavoidably to a bourgeois constitutional state. And

Nicholas confirmed that he understood only political extremes: either absolute monarchy or a democratic republic, for constitutional monarchy struck him as something false and ambiguous. Preservation of the Russian autocracy in full inviolability he considered his first and most important obligation.

It remains to define the relations between the government and the nobility. Nicholas's government set itself a dual task: to resurrect the social power of the nobility and to fashion it into a tool of governmental administration. The first goal had to be pursued by the adoption of measures aimed at purging this "most important" class of all its degenerate elements by either assisting them or eliminating them. The government developed a unique migration policy, providing impoverished noble families with government land beyond the Volga River or in Siberia and with grants from the treasury to help them get established. But, on the other hand, the government placed the children of noble families which were hopelessly degraded, both economically and culturally, in cantonist (military reservation) schools, while the half-educated adult males in such families were sent into military service without their noble privileges. The government endeavored to enhance the importance of provincial and district noble assemblies by further increasing their right to participate in elections, by giving them the responsibility for selecting chairmen of judicial chambers, and by summoning them to special activity in the management of local affairs with the right to direct appeals to higher authorities concerning their own class or local needs in general. In return, the nobility was obliged to assume the role of an obedient and industrious instrument of administration. The elected representatives of the nobility were only another variety of governmental bureaucrat, and their service was comparable to state service. The marshals of the nobility — through a whole series of "committees" dealing with roads, responsibility for manorial administration, the mustering of recruits, public food supplies, the struggle against epidemics, and the like — became assistants to the provincial authorities in local administration.

What was called the system of "noble self-government" formed part of the structure of bureaucratic organs of the government. The government also persistently supported the class nature of the social order by measures regarding public education. The selection of students enrolled in schools was determined by a series of steps in such a way that on one "could strive to elevate himself above that condition in which he was judged to belong." Secondary and especially higher education were reserved for the children of "nobles and government functionaries." But even here the entire policy was directed toward subjecting education to the conservative views of the government with a decisive curtailment of its breadth and freedom of development, aimed at subordinating the educational mission of the school to the goal of rendering public opinion politically harmless.

The reactionary measures for rebuilding the rotted foundations of a state system based upon social class were too artificial for strong and solid results. They could not stop the course of evolution, but merely delay it. Within the confines of the old order, Russian life was following its own ways in direct contradiction to the conservative principles of government policy. The economy had entered new paths of commercial and industrial development. International economic ties were becoming stronger. During Nicholas's reign, Russian exports increased from 75 to 230 million rubles, and imports from 52 to 200 million rubles in value. The growth of foreign trade necessitated a reexamination of tariffs in view of the competition with American raw materials in European markets and to accommodate tariff rates to the customs union of the Kingdom of Poland and Russia. The dependence of Russian economic life upon general European economic relations grew stronger and more complex. The question of the role of foreign investment in the development of Russian capitalism, especially in connection with the problem of railroad construction, became imminent. In the south, a significant sugar-beet industry arose (the first factory was established in 1802; by 1845 there were

206 of them), the physiognomy of the central Russian industrial area took shape, which increasingly lived on grain pur-
chased from the agricultural provinces. Serfdom declined and
decayed, and even the proportion of privately-owned serfs in
the general population diminished (from 45 to 37.5 percent).
The middle social strata grew stronger. Despite governmental measures, the heterogeneous social composition of students
in the *gymnasia* and universities increased, and by the end of
Nicholas's reign the Russian intelligentsia had in large measure
lost its noble class character and was becoming petty bourgeois
and multi-class. "Public life" obviously no longer was confined
to limits which were maintained vigorously by the government.

Even the policies of the government itself were not so narrowly constrained. It was essential to take into account the
new requirements of the country, to support and protect them.
And Nicholas I personally reflected these new, developing tendencies of Russian life in his own interests and attitudes. He
was deeply intrigued by questions of technology, technical education, new enterprises, and a broader statement of questions
of economic and financial policy. Working with the efficient
but extremely cautious and deeply conservative Kankrin,[8] Nicholas was bolder than his own Minister of Finance, who looked upon the penetration of Russia by foreign capital with exaggerated caution (asserting that "each nation must strive for
full independence from other nations") and considered that
the time was not yet ripe for the building of railroads in Russia. He proceeded from the idea that Russia was an exclusively
agricultural country where, of course, it was necessary to protect industries, primarily the extractive ones, but cautiously,
with "homeopathic doses." Both men zealously fostered higher and secondary technical education in Russia. "We are crown-
ing the work of Peter," Nicholas boasted. Groups of young
scholars were sent on missions to study Western science and,
greatly energized thereby, to teach at Moscow University and
other higher educational institutions and to redevelop Russian
scientific literature. The results of this effort were in one

respect more pre-Petrine than Petrine. Western ideas and concepts evoked acute mistrust and intense surveillance through the censorship, not only of books but of lectures. Entire fields of learning were excluded from instruction and efforts were made forcibly to guide the general tenor of scholarly endeavor in the spirit of "the outlook of the government" and official, patriotic doctrines. Nicholas wished all cultural activity to be subordinated to a strict, barracks discipline. The order and forms of the military system were spread to "the corps of communications engineers" or to "the forestry corps;" and the university statute of 1835 raised the problem of "bringing our universities closer to the fundamental and salutary principles of Russian administration" and of introducing into the universities "the order of military service and in general a strict observation of established forms, the principle of rank, and precision in the fulfillment of even the simplest orders." It was not for nothing that a majority of statesmen under Nicholas I came from a military background, and even the secular administration of the Russian Orthodox Church was directed by an adjutant-general who had formerly served as commander of a Hussar regiment of palace guards.

The urge to pour new wine into old bottles in so moderate an amount that the bottles would not overflow, and to use all the forces of authority to bolster antiquated forms against the pressure of new contents was characteristic of Nicholas's politics. The more or less clear understanding that a developing internal crisis urgently required creative work paralyzed the autocracy in its own peculiar way, at such historic moments, by an "inability to help itself, without repudiating its very essence" (in the words of E.V. Tarle[9]). In Nicholas's reign the very foundations of those social relations upon which the autocracy had developed, and with which it was connected by unbreakable historical bonds, decayed. As the ground under it became less firm, the autocracy attempted to make use of the last remaining possibilities of the antiquated system, now restoring shattered elements, now straining to the breaking point the old methods of administration and government. The autocracy continued "permanently" only to the extent that its innovations were socially and politically harmless. With keen mistrust of social forces — the conservative ones because of their degeneration, the progressive ones because of their "revolutionary" nature, however imaginary — the government endeavored to live a self-contained life, apart from and above society, resulting in the personal military-political dictatorship of the emperor.

CHAPTER IV

THE WEAKNESS OF
AUTHORITY

Nicholas I undoubtedly expended
much effort and time on state administration and tried to direct it
personally and actively. He had
neither respect nor trust for the
system of bureaucratic institutions bequeathed by Catherine II
and Alexander I. He knew all too well the inherent weakness
of the bureaucratic apparatus and the profound depravity of
the bureaucracy itself. Dissatisfaction with a system that was
badly adjusted and quite disordered, and mistrust of individuals and of social groups: these were the psychological bases of
Nicholas's despotism. All independence of thought and action
seemed to him inadmissible "arrogance and opposition," and
all hope lay in stringent execution of orders and in unquestioning obedience. He regarded his ministers as mere executors of
his will, not as plenipotentiary and responsible directors of distinct departments.

The broadly developing system of ministerial reports "in
the name of the Emperor" on the most varied questions permitted the emperor to play the part of the supreme authority,
directly in command of the country. He regarded it as his obligation to resolve personally all sorts of important issues and
problems. He took his own competence for granted. Nicholas,
like Suvorov,[1] would not recognize "inability" in matters of
service, and indeed he looked upon his entire life, including his
governmental activity, as service. He cultivated a great self-sufficiency and decided all questions with brief and irrevocable

commands. As ruler he viewed himself as versed in all matters, "as should be anyone in his position." The tale is told of how he approached the first state budget presented for his approval by the Minister of Finance. Nicholas paid close attention to it, examined every estimated expenditure and personally corrected a series of figures. All of this was done, of course, at first sight, at his own discretion and momentary inspiration. The entire construction of the budget proved to be disordered and confused. The minister had to explain to the monarch, much as one might talk to a man in the street, that one couldn't manage state finances this way, and to present for approval another copy of the estimates, free of diligent but arbitrary corrections.

As time passed, Nicholas gained much knowledge and mastered many skills, comprehended much on his own, participated in committees dealing with various questions, and worked assiduously on his own solutions. But the actual decision was always reserved for himself, as autocrat. In essence, he personally directed his own policies. "He performed conscientiously, according to his own convictions; these convictions were a heavy burden for the sins of Russia," wrote a thoughtful contemporary, V. S. Aksakova,[2] at the time of Nicholas's death. When more complex questions arose, especially concerning more or less essential reforms, the projects were transmitted for discussion to committees composed of trusted individuals, selected personally by the emperor. He followed the course of the discussion, influenced it by communicating his own opinions, but grew ever more accustomed to that spirit of conservatism, that extreme restraint in the face of any sort of basically new undertakings, which increasingly led to a fruitless outcome of the committee's deliberations. If innovations were decided upon, the proposed measures usually were implemented in experimental form is some region of the state, and subsequently introduced in the State Council in the form of a legislative proposal which in essence had already been approved by the sovereign, and then simply confirmed, apart from the Council, by a resolution attached to the report

GRAND DUKE NICHOLAS PAVLOVICH

of a minister. These resolutions on reports, sometimes highly detailed and filled with justifications, sometimes brief and peremptory, concerning general or very specific questions, elucidated for the bureaucracy the views of the sovereign on one question or another and provided the basis for resolving similar matters.

This was the unique, personal legislation of the emperor, which inevitably had a fragmentary and haphazard character. Cropping up on one occasion or another, it transformed the activity of the higher authorities from generally planned efforts to largely uncoordinated decrees. And among the higher bureaucracy there were many who did not approve of such a method of operation by the bearer of supreme power. Nicholas was reproached for the fact that he ruled unsystematically, destroying through his personal interference any regularity in the system of administration, and for the fact that he forgot that the business of the sovereign is ruling and not administering, general leadership and not current management. Under Nicholas could be seen especially clearly that characteristic of autocracy which Alexander I had denounced, that commands were given "more on an *ad hoc* basis than for general reasons of state," and had "neither a relationship to one another, nor a unity of purpose, nor a constancy of operation." But Nicholas regarded government by personal will and personal outlook to be the direct obligation of the autocrat. General and specific questions, matters of national significance and the fates of private individuals, all completely depended upon the personal discretion and sentiment of the sovereign. Sometimes he was guided in his decisions by legal precedents, but more often by his personal opinions, suggesting that "the best theory of law is good morality."

The autocratic principle of personal rule of the state, apart from established institutions, received particular expression in the very structure of the central administration, thanks to the primacy of "His Majesty's Own Chancery,"[3] the most direct agency of personal imperial authority. In the very first year of his reign, Nicholas placed under the jurisdiction of his Chancery all legislative matters, having established for this purpose a special ("Second") section of it. Here all the work on the "complete collection" and the "code of laws"[4] was carried out; and if, according to Speransky's[5] thought, this was merely preparation for a further task — the reworking of the collected and systematized material into a new code of laws — then the essential conservatism of the supreme authority brought to a standstill all work on the code (excluding the "Code of Punishments"). In the Second Section all general legislative work was carried on and, more importantly, exemptions from laws and changes in them on various grounds 'in the system of the higher administration" were sought and obtained through this section. The immediate superintendence of his Chancery was entrusted by Nicholas to a supreme police force and for this purpose the famous Third Section was established, and with it a "special corps of gendarmes" with the division of the entire country into five (later eight) gendarme districts. Further, along with the Fourth Section, which directed the so-called "Institutions of the Empress Maria,"[6] there arose special temporary sections of His Majesty's Own Chancery and various committees attached to it, for the study of various important questions such as the conditions of the state peasants, the administration of the Kingdom of Poland and of the Caucasus, and so on.

All of these Sections were fully empowered organs of "extraordinary" administration, through which the supreme authority of the autocrat operated apart from the regular system of governmental institutions. Of these, the Third Section received special significance, in the full spirit of a protective and investigative authority. It was in charge of the "supreme police," but it interpreted this very broadly. Along with the search for "state criminals" (and what wasn't included in that category!), numerous additional powers and responsibilities were concentrated in the Third Section. Prison sentences and terms of exile were under its supervision. It collected all sorts of data and information about "suspicious persons," not only in a political sense but criminal as well; secret measures of surveillance and deportation were launched against such persons by the Third Section. It also conducted surveillance of all foreigners and all Russians who returned from abroad. From all provinces and gendarme districts it received periodic "reports" on all sorts of incidents and on the most noteworthy criminal cases, especially those concerning counterfeiters, bootleggers, and smugglers. It closely followed peasant disturbances, investigated their origins and causes, and took measures to eradicate them. It amplified the scrutiny of literature, inasmuch as the censorship department, whose obligation it was to "guide public opinion in harmony with the present political circumstances and views of the government," itself was placed under the strict supervision and direction of the Third Section, and beginning in 1828 theatrical censorship was transferred entirely to it as well. The dream of the Third Section was that it — and through it its head, the emperor — should be aware of everything significant, from a police point of view, that occurred in every corner of the empire. A constant influx of information was provided by the reports from the gendarme districts and the general administration. All this motley material was reported to Nicholas and absorbed much of his attention and often his energetic, direct participation. When "imperial" resolutions required additional information on one or another occurrence, gendarme officers were sent out (Nicholas knew them well and often indicated which should be in charge) with special powers to conduct investigations on the spot or to take extraordinary measures "upon imperial command."

The Third Section and the Corps of Gendarmes were powerful sources of personal information for the sovereign about everything which happened in the country, and were instruments of his personal supervision of the system and conduct of both the administration and of the man in the street. Nicholas read reports carefully (so carefully that he even corrected errors), and went deeply into reports not only concerning major

events which had social significance, but also concerning the
escapades and adventures of individuals who were under police surveillance for the most varied reasons. He went into details, demanding further surveillance and new facts, inquiries
by provinces and information by ministries. He ascertained
blame and personally meted out punishment to the guilty,
only occasionally ordering that they be prosecuted. Nicholas
considered himself the guardian of order and the trustee of
good general morality, and he punished those who destroyed
order and morality by using administrative exile, for which he
himself often personally selected the actual place of exile
(Viatka, Sol'vychegodsk, Kargopol, and so on, and Solovki
for incorrigible recidivists), by making them soldiers or fortress
prisoners, or even by sending them to "madhouses." This last
punishment often was applied in the most terrible way: "mad-
men, exiled to have their minds corrected," were an everyday
occurrence, along with "state convicts."

The more complex or serious cases were transferred to
military or civil courts and sent to judicial institutions with
the suggestion that they be decided immediately, without wait-
ing their turn, or that they be sent for investigation to the Ministers of Justice and Internal Affairs or to the local governor
and marshal of the nobility who would consult with the district
gendarme staff-officer. The broad intelligence system of the
Third Section was used by Nicholas to verify the information
gathered by his ministers in their own spheres of jurisdiction,
and he often directed their attention to various irregularities.

The activity of the Third Section naturally led to a broad
use of denunciations and individual complaints. More than a
few voluntary informers were found in all sorts of cases. The
ancient *Lèse-Majesté* was resurrected in the form of a declaration on "important state secrets," about which informers
could advise only the sovereign himself. Nicholas by no means
disregarded such declarations. He summoned informers to
St. Petersburg, entrusted their interrogation to the Third Section, and if they were persistent he wrote to them personally

and gave monetary rewards, although some of them who made
obviously ridiculous and malicious allegations were arrested,
exiled, or even sent to insane asylums as punishment for their
malice and for the trouble they caused. Through the Third
Section the emperor entered into the private affairs of his subjects, looked into their complaints of injustices and oppression,
quarrels over inheritances and complicated family dissension,
chastised children for disrespect toward their parents, placed
fathers under trusteeship for squandering family property, as-
sisted in the recovery of debts, and the like. Just as in St.
Petersburg Nicholas loved to appear unexpectedly at government offices early in the morning to see if the bureaucrats were
on the job and if all affairs were in order, so he endeavored,
through his gendarmes, to play the master who peeked into
every corner of Russian life and to hold it in trust. Since he
himself lacked the time to be everywhere, he substituted his
faithful servitors.

The Third Section and the Corps of Gendarmes were de-
signed to break down the bureaucratic wall between the autocracy and the people. Nicholas sought in this way to achieve
popularity and trust. These new institutions were put forth as
something beneficial to the "loyal" inhabitants and dependent
upon their support. Instructions to the Corps of Gendarmes
made it incumbent upon them to uncover abuses and nip them
in the bud, to defend the populace against oppression and ex-
tortion on the part of the bureaucracy, to seek out and recom-
mend for reward "most loyal and humble servants" and even
to "engender a striving for goodness in those who have strayed
and lead them upon the true path." Gendarme officers were
to seek the trust of all strata of society and to inspire the population with confidence that, through them, "the voice of every
citizen can reach the throne of the Tsar." A broad canvas was
unrolled which depicted centralized police supervision operating on a statewide scale, assuming an active trusteeship, diligent
in the gathering of information and imperiously responsive to
even the slightest, most mundane events and deeds.

The general goals of this system were those of the police and the political regime. Under the personal leadership of the sovereign, a struggle was waged against the mounting social discontent of all classes of the population, using two methods: severe repression of all its manifestations and certain ameliorations of its causes, insofar as this did not require any fundamental alterations of the existing order. Mercilessly suppressing peasant uprisings and dealing sternly with "instigators," Nicholas demanded investigation of complaints of the cruelty or dissoluteness of masters and of their excessive exploitation of serfs, and in extreme cases he ordered that their estates be placed under trusteeship, sometimes with the arrest of the villainous master and his banishment from his estate. Exile to the various corners of the empire, forced military service in the Caucasus or in frontier battalions, and sometimes even incarceration in "madhouses" were used also to punish displays of free thinking, such as the composition of "unrestrained" poems and "suspicious" documents or imprudent and critical remarks addressed to the higher authorities. Nicholas's government was extremely sensitive to the slightest sign of disrespect and censure, and considered any sort of criticism inappropriate. It sought to inspire the population with unconditional trust in governmental authority and with the conviction that "shortcomings will be met and abuses will be corrected not by wild and always destructive dreams but, gradually, by the established authority above." The heavy atmosphere of hypocrisy and arbitrariness ever more tightly shrouded this supreme authority, caught up in the illusion of its own power, apart from and above real life.

The Third Section was only the most visible and obvious manifestation of Nicholas's political system. The military style of the Corps of Gendarmes, the principle of discipline, of immediate and unconditional obedience, of personal command and unquestioning execution of the orders of the chief commandant in a system of delegated missions — all of these methods were adopted by Nicholas I on a statewide scale.

Nicholas built his entire government according to military form, and it was not in vain that he called the state "his command."

The closest circle of advisors to the sovereign in governmental matters were his "imperial general headquarters," the ranks of his "royal retinue," a tight group of people carefully chosen and closely screened (a significant percentage of them from the Baltic nobility), people who were faithful, reliable, obedient, and loyal. Nicholas remained intimate with and gracious toward his adjutant-generals and aides-de-camp, but he often severely punished them for even comparatively minor faults. Skeptical and suspicious, he trusted the members of his own retinue, seeing them as people who knew his views and desires and who were ready without question to translate them into reality, not from fear but from conviction. Whereever he wished to have personal supervision and good management, he sent his adjutant-generals and aides-de-camp. They had to be constantly prepared to depart on the most varied and often delicate missions. Through them Nicholas kept the administration of the army in his own hands, sending them on military inspections, to supervise the mustering of recruits, and the like. He sent them to investigate irregularities in the military and civilian financial management, requiring that detailed reports be submitted to him personally. Such missions were a constant means of direct interference by the sovereign in all matters and questions: in the investigation of the actions of civil and military authorities, in important criminal matters or especially complex civil cases, in measures for the relief of provincial populations suffering from famine ("to provide the inhabitants with a new sign of His Majesty's unceasing concern and personal attention toward those whom disaster has befallen"), in the struggle against outbreaks of fires, in which could be seen the work of arsonists, and the like.

The adjutants in his retinue were the "closest servitors" of the emperor, by analogy with whom he called the state secretaries his "civil adjutants-general." Finding them free

POLICE RUSSE.

of the hated "arrogance and opposition," Nicholas at the same time required of them that many-sided competence which he ascribed to himself in his own work. If one of his adjutant-generals directed the governmental department dealing with church affairs, imperiously deciding canonical and even theological questions, then why not send another to Munich to look into the completion of an order for a "painted picture"? All of these matters were subjected to the imperious instructions of the autocratic will. Thus did Nicholas himself deal with the artistic treasures of the Hermitage: he submitted them to political censorship, ordering the removal of portraits of Polish leaders and Decembrists from the collections and the "destruction of this simian," the portrait of Voltaire by Gudonov. He applied his own Philistine artistic taste, demanding the destruction or sale of many paintings "because of their worthlessness."

The personal retinue of members of the sovereign's suite became the *Oprichnina*[7] of Nicholas I, separated not only from society but even from those in regular state service. From them he chose candidates for responsible state positions, concentrating the entire administration of the state in the hands of his "own" people. By such a system Nicholas sought to emancipate himself both from self-serving bureaucratic routines and from the demands of the nobility, and to observe the course of life more distinctly and influence it more directly. Did he deceive himself with regard to the results? Hardly. The doleful quotation attributed to him, that "Russia is governed by bureau chiefs," indicates that the weakness of authority was no secret to him. He nearly relinquished his influence upon the life of the country and buried himself in the defense of "order." To preserve inviolably his autocracy and to delay the victory of new currents of life as much as possible — that was his entire, hopeless task. "The strange thing about this ruler," Countess Nesselrode[8] wrote, "is that he ploughs his vast realm, but not a single fruit-bearing seed does he sow."

The state apparatus degenerated, losing its defined social content. The empire experienced a protracted state of un-stable equilibrium between the old and the new, between the decaying and the developing aspects of the national economy and socio-political life. The existing political form became an end in itself for the preservation of its own authority. But this authority had at its disposal the vast reserve of organized state energy, the significant personal forces of the country, and could not help but display itself in activities which would justify its great importance. Never before had the pretentious self-sufficiency of this authority been raised so high in Russia as during the reign of Nicholas I. It sought to absorb and em-body the entire community.

The whole philosophy of this system was successfully formulated by Ya. I. Rostovtsev in the previously-mentioned doctrine of supreme authority as something of a focal point of social life, corresponding to the conscience in the personal life of an individual, which demands the authoritative estab-lishment of a "moral order" in society so as not to perish in the conflict of varied individual impulses. Individuals are united in society, according to this theory, only by obedience to authority. Such was the understanding of the life of the country in the reign of Paul, who forbade the use of the word "society," requiring instead the use of the word "state." And (in the words of Liubimov, the friend and panegyrist of such a pillar of Russian conservatism as M.N. Katkov[9]), the "state idea took the exclusive form of command; in command were combined law, justice, mercy, and punishment," in the Nichol-aevan era. Nicholas attempted to reduce the authority of the state to the personal autocracy of the "father-commander," in the manner of a military command, imbued, in the com-mon spirit of the era, by a patriarchal and proprietary, serf-owning conception of all relations of power and government. According to the official doctrine effectively formulated by

the Minister of Public Instruction, S.S. Uvarov, at the basis of
original Russian life lay three principles: Autocracy, Orthodoxy, and Nationality.

The first facet of this trinity, assuredly the predominant
one, is, of course, Autocracy, to which all else must submit,
not only externally but internally as well, not only from fear
but as a matter of conscience. Orthodoxy, one of the supports
of this authority, was seen not as that "internal truth" of an
independent and authoritative Russian Church, about which
the Slavophiles[10] dreamed, but as a completely practicable
system of Church domination over the spiritual life of the
"flock" and as a tool of political force of the autocracy, completely submissive to civil authority under the administration
of the Procurator of the Holy Synod. The word "Nationality"
was understood to mean official patriotism, unconditional ad-
miration for governmental Russia, for its military strength and
police power, for Russia in its official aspect, "in the contrast
of Russia-on-paper with Russia-in-nature," according to the
expression of the nationalistic historian, M.P. Pogodin.[11] It
also meant admiration for a Russia decorated in the official
style, hypocritically confident of its power, of in incorrupti-
bility of its ways, and intentionally closing its eyes to enormous public and state needs.

In the domestic life of Russia, this system of "official
nationality" was embodied in a complete stagnation of organic,
creative activity and concealed the agony of the decaying old
order. In international relations it led to presumptuous acts,
to political adventurism which, by overtaxing the forces of a
country already shaken by internal crisis, lured the regime toward a fatal catastrophe.

CHAPTER V

RUSSIA AND EUROPE

Throughout the entire reign of Nicholas I, the Ministry of Foreign Affairs was administered by Count Karl Nesselrode.[1] Stein,[2] the great patriot of a unified Germany and the exponent of the national idea, spoke of him extremely harshly: "He has neither a fatherland nor a native tongue, and this is of great significance; he has not a single basic feeling; his father was a German adventurer, his mother is unknown, he himself was educated in Berlin and serves in Moscow." He was the type of German servitor who came from a petty German principality but chose the spaciousness of a foreign career. The son of a Catholic and a Jewess who converted to Protestantism, he happened to have been baptized as an Anglican. He was educated in Berlin in the spirit of fashionable French culture. Through his father's service, he early became connected with the Russian court. At the age of sixteen he was an aide-de-camp to the Emperor Paul and at the age of twenty he was a chamberlain, rapidly making a career for himself at court. Under Alexander I he was a diplomat entrusted with special missions, an instrument of the personal policy of the emperor for secret relations with the betrayers of Napoleon, Talleyrand and Caulaincourt, and from 1816 he was Alexander's State Secretary for diplomatic affairs. During the period when Russian foreign policy wavered between the general European tendencies of the Congress Era and Russian interests in Eastern Europe, Nesselrode was the vehicle of the former just as another State Secretary, Capodistrias,[3] was the vehicle of the latter, because of their connection with his Greek patriotism.

The change in the direction of a more independent Russian policy in the Eastern Question, which occurred toward the end of Alexander's reign and was adopted by Nicholas, was formulated by Nesselrode in his first report to the new emperor, where the general European questions and immediate interests of Russia were skillfully delimited. Nicholas fulfilled the demand of his brother Constantine, stated during their celebrated dealings concerning the fate of the Russian throne, in the form of his advice to keep Nesselrode as a representative of the legacy of Alexander. And he remained under Nicholas as a bearer of the traditions of the Congress Era, of the "politics of principles," which assigned Russia the role of a force for the preservation of the monarchical order in Europe and of those forms of "political equilibrium" which were established at the Congress of Vienna. Nicholas valued these principles of Frederick William III and Alexander I, and he valued Nesselrode, as well, as a convenient and experienced colleague. He read Nesselrode's reports attentively and learned from him, but in actual fact Nicholas conducted his own policy. Nesselrode did not really exaggerate when he called himself a "modest instrument of [Nicholas's] designs and an organ of his political plans." Nesselrode became Vice Chancellor and Chancellor of State of the Russian Empire, but he remained all the same State Secretary for diplomatic affairs.

The relationship between Russia and Europe took on a new character in the second quarter of the nineteenth century. A strong reaction against the internationalism of Alexander I developed and gained the upper hand even during his own reign. The tendency to isolate Russia from Europe was strengthened. The policy of Alexander I struck too painfully at the interests which prevailed in Russia. And the problems connected with them became especially aggravated in the cases of Poland and the Near East.

MANŒUVRES AU CHAMP DE MARS.

The incorporation of the Duchy of Warsaw markedly complicated Western relations with Russia. The Polish lands had had long and geographically determined relations with Prussia. Polish exports and the Polish market for the sale of imported goods provided an advantageous objective of Prussian exploitation. The favorable terms established at the Congress of Vienna and in subsequent agreements for the exchange of goods between the parts of divided Poland guaranteed these Prussian advantages for the future, and acquired an extremely broad significance, on the one hand, because they embraced the former Polish lands "according to the borders of 1772," and, on the other hand, because Prussia was also backed by the German tariff union. Prussia endeavored to utilize these conditions to capture Polish and Russian markets for the advantage of her own commerce and industry. Tariff barriers were erected in turn by Russia and Poland and led to a new triumph of the protective system in Russian imperial economic policy. It also had another, no less significant result: the economic drawing together of the Kingdom of Poland and Russia and the weakening and later complete abolition of Russian-Polish border customs, on the initiative not of Russian but of Polish financial leaders, headed by Xavier Lubecki.[4]

All of these economic relations, which can be only mentioned in passing here,* significantly complicated the problem of the independence of the Kingdom of Poland within the Russian Empire. Questions of imperial policy increasingly overwhelmed it — and not only tariff, commercial, industrial, or financial questions. Nicholas approached the Polish problem also from a political and strategic perspective. The western borders of the empire seemed to him to have been weakened, not strengthened, by the incorporation of the Kingdom of Poland. Completely disregarding, with his Russian imperial

*See my article "Economics and Politics in the Polish Question at the Beginning of the 19th Century" in the journal *Bor'ba Klassov* [The Struggle of Classes], Volume I. — *Author's Note*

point of view, the fate of Polish nationality, he would have preferred another partition of Poland, with the borders of the empire on the rivers Narew and Vistula and with the cessation of lands to the west of this border to neighboring powers, possibly in exchange for Eastern Galicia, but this was in vain. The independent existence of constitutional Poland was incompatible with the entire tenor of his outlook. He regarded its creation as an error on Alexander's part, as "regretable" as the constitutional promises made by Frederick William III to his subjects; on these points Nicholas decisively backed away from his reverential esteem for his favorite authorities. He was completely negative toward the principle of national self-determination. The connection between national movements and liberal and liberationist ones endowed the principle with a revolutionary character. This was an anti-monarchical principle, incompatible with the idea of autocracy. The call for a rebirth of nationality, proceeding from the arena of active political life, seemed only a pretext, only a form of revolutionary agitation. This was the source, for example, of the hostile attitude of Nicholas's government toward Pan-Slavism and suspicion of the Slavophiles. It was explained officially that Russian patriotism had to derive "not from Slavdom, an invention of fantasy, but from the Russian principle, without any traces of contemporary political ideas."

The Polish uprising of 1830-31 served Nicholas as a vivid confirmation of these views of his. Russia herself had created the Polish forces which now came into conflict with her. Polish finances (restored by Lubecki) "were permitted to be converted within the Treasury into a reserve fund, which proved to be sufficient for the support of the present struggle," Nicholas noted in his own handwritten memorandum on the Polish uprising. "The army, created in the Imperial image, was entirely supplied by Russia," and was very well organized on the basis of the Russian cadres. Polish industry was elevated, at Russian expense, in the imperial market. And the internal

autonomy of Poland, which many considered to be permissible
and even praiseworthy there but acknowledged to be criminal
and punished in the empire, undermined "that which constitutes the strength of the Empire, that is, the conviction that it
can be powerful and great only under the monarchical rule of
an autocratic sovereign."

The Polish uprising greatly worried Nicholas, and cost
him "ten months of torture," from which he thanked Paskevich[5] for delivering him. But the worry remained. It was necessary to put an end to Poland. Unconcealed joy resounds in
the words of Nicholas: "I received a reliquary with the remains
of the constitution, for which I am very thankful; it will be
laid to rest in the Armory." He replaced the "deceased" with
the abortive "Organic Statute," which transformed the Kingdom of Poland into an imperial province, and in reality placed
it under the military and policy dictatorship of vice-regents
and contemplated, in order to undermine the influence of the
landowning *Szlachta,* "the emancipation of the peasants of
the Kingdom according to the example provided by Prussia."
Nicholas's ideal would have been the utter Russification of
Poland in order to unify the entire empire, with its Polish, German, Ukrainian, and other borderlands, on the principles of
autocratic authority and "official nationality."

But in Polish policy it was necessary to take neighboring
countries into account. Nicholas was extremely displeased by
the mistakes which Frederick William IV had made with the
Poles of Poznan and in the national and religious questions,
and he tried both personally and through his wife, the empress,
to exert influence upon her brother to bring his Polish policy
into agreement with Nicholas's national program of suppressing Polish life. He was also displeased with the actions of the
Austrian government in Galicia. He suggested that concerted
action by the three governments might eradicate Polish nationalism, and did not at all recognize the degree to which his
policy of repression served only to strengthen the patriotism

of the Poles. His Polish impressions and worries undoubtedly
strengthened Nicholas's conservatism and increased his conviction that his political system was uniquely capable of pre-
serving "tranquility and order" in the Russian Empire, and
even its very existence.

Danger threatened these "foundations" primarily from
the West. The West had suffered far deeper revolutionary
shocks and had degenerated at the very roots of its existence.
Russia's ties with Europe had been strengthened, and the processes of general European evolution were ever more deeply
evidenced in Russia's way of life. The wheel of Russian history could be stopped only if the fatal motion of Europe could
be arrested or at least delayed. Throughout his life, Nicholas
waged a contest against the "spirit of the times" that was beyond his strength.

This struggle for "principle" and "tradition" became
peculiarly entangled with his ideas of Russia's international
interests. From his brother Alexander and from his Prussian
father-in-law he firmly mastered the meaning of "legitimate"
authority, legitimate in the source of its right to rule. Hereditary monarchical authority had to be a "sacred trust" in the
hands of its bearer, which even law could not diminish or
share with representatives of the people. The curious episode
of Frederick William III's will, which Nicholas had helped
compose and which gave members of the dynasty the right to
protest any effort by its head to diminish the sovereign authority through constitutional experiments, is quite indicative. It
gave Nicholas an additional opportunity to attempt to inter-
vene in the internal affairs of Prussia. Using his personal intimacy with the Prussian king, Nicholas tried to restrain him
from cowardly efforts at playing the liberal and from convok-
ing the "general ranks" and acknowledging their right to vote
on financial questions, especially in the matter of state loans.
He valued Prussia's friendship. "But," he wrote to Frederick
William, "Russia always will be the true ally of its old friend —

good, old, and loyal Prussia," but not of a new Prussia which
would make compromise with "revolution." He needed the
old, military-feudal, monarchical Prussia as a bulwark against
the revolutionary West, and not a Prussia which was lured by
the growth of trade and industrial capitalism onto new paths
of political development. This nascent new Prussia was painfully attempting to exploit not only Poland, but even Russia,
as its *Hinterland*, for its own commercial advantages.

Following the shocks of 1848 and the attempt to make
Frederick William the head of a united Germany, Nicholas
was prepared for a break with Prussia if the latter threw itself
into the arms of a new Germany, a "federally united, democratic, aggressive Germany, thirsty for supremacy and terri-
torial conquests." The bourgeois-revolutionary upheaval in
Germany alarmed Nicholas not only as the ruination of the
old order, based upon the absolutism of monarchical authority, but also as the source of a terrible capitalistic imperialism
in international relations. And, with all the force of his influence, he tried to suppress these tendencies, in opposition to
the unification of Germany, in support of Denmark against
Prussia in the Schleswig-Holstein question, in support of Austria and the secondary German states against Prussia in matters
of pan-Germanic organization. The defense of "principles of
order" took on the fully realistic meaning of a struggle against
the rise of national powers which endangered the international
position of the Russian Empire. In a new form it revived the
old politics of the eighteenth century: divided and weak
neighbors were much more convenient.

Nicholas viewed the revolutionary movement in the Austrian lands as no less a danger. The Habsburg Monarchy, the
age-old bulwark of the old order, had to be preserved. The
Hungarian revolution was understood by Nicholas as a great
danger because of the conspicuous participation of Poles in it.
The success of this revolt would have threatened a new growth
of the Polish movement, which had erupted continuously
throughout the 1840's and to which Nicholas had dealt a

telling blow in 1846, having insisted on the elimination of the
"freedom" of Cracow.[6] The suppression of the Hungarian
revolt by Russian armies in 1849 was an act of self-preservation on Nicholas's part, an aspect of his personal policy and
not a service to an ally, as it was often portrayed both officially and unofficially.

Nicholas brought this instinct for self-preservation to
bear throughout his general European defensive policy. Western journalism was correct when it saw the Russian autocrat
as the chief enemy of the revolutionary renewal of Europe
(an idea which was so persistently elaborated by Karl Marx in
a series of fiery articles). Clearly, Nicholas followed the source
of all revolutionary shocks, France, with particular anxiety.
Foreseeing an inevitable explosion, he judged the ultra-react-
ionary measures of Charles X to be too harsh, but his fall and
the transfer of power to Louis Philippe was taken by Nicholas
as a challenge to the remnants of the "old order." "He attempted to wreck and ruin my position as Russian Emperor,"
said Nicholas about Louis Philippe, "and I will never forgive
him for this."

Authority which had been created by a revolution and
which saw its legitimacy in the "will of the people" could not
be recognized as "legitimate;" its legitimization by international recognition would undermine all the foundations of
"order." This was Nicholas's primary thought. The recent
events of the Napoleonic era made him think that the revolutionary outburst had unleashed a mass of nationalistic energy
in the country and threatened to overturn all international relations through an active foreign policy. Nicholas greeted the
new authority in France with hostility. Impulsively he ordered
all Russians to leave France, forbade the display of the French
tricolored flag in Russian ports, and did not want to recognize
the "usurper." This meant a break in diplomatic and trade relations with France. With difficulty the Russian envoy in Paris,
Pozzo di Borgo,[7] succeeded in explaining to his angry monarch

the conservative character of the monarchy of Louis Philippe, as an expedient means of suspending the revolutionary movement, whose elimination would lead to the overthrow of monarchy and the proclamation of a republic. The recognition of Louis Philippe by other powers made Nicholas yield and restrict himself to politically tactless slights of the king, whom he absolutely refused to recognize as the equal of genuine sovereigns. This feeling was so strong in Nicholas that he even gloated over the fall of the monarchy of Louis Philippe in 1848: the "scoundrel," as the king was in Nicholas's opinion, had lost his power in the very same way he had gained it, and he had only gotten what he deserved.

This attitude toward Louis Philippe was reenforced by the Polish sympathies of France and by the reverberations of the July revolution throughout Europe. Nicholas was particularly outraged by the division of the Netherlands into Belgium and Holland; he pressed for military defense by other powers of the "rights" of the King of the Netherlands and prepared the Russian army for this action. But the independence of Belgium had the support of England and France; Prussia and Austria remained passive: it was necessary to retreat even here. All these retreats were then covered by the foreign office myths of which Nesselrode was master, such as the recognition of Louis Philippe as the deputy of Charles X, upon whose abdication the former would receive full power; or the recognition of Belgium when the King of the Netherlands recognized that state, and the like.

Concessions of this nature weighed heavily upon Nicholas. They formed further steps in the decomposition of those "foundations of order" over which he tried to stand guard. The system of the Congress of Vienna and the force of the treaties of 1815 were finally shattered. They were replaced by a core of agreements made in 1833-35, to which Nicholas held firm, although he was already without much confidence in the stability of "order" in Europe. The tsar's government persistently supported diplomatic myths until the very end:

EMPEROR NICHOLAS, TSAREVICH ALEXANDER, EMPRESS ALEXANDRA

Russian diplomacy continued to refer to "the treaties of 1815."
The events of 1848 struck a new blow against the Nicholaevan
"system." Once again France rushed toward a new future.
The Republican government declared the treaties of 1815 to
be void; the National Assembly proclaimed the leading principles of French policy to be alliance with Germany, the independence of Poland, and the liberation of Italy. This was a
direct challenge.

"The solemn moment had come which I had been pre-
dicting for eighteen years; the revolution has arisen from the
ashes and threatens our mutual existence with inevitable
danger," wrote Nicholas to the King of Prussia regarding the
February Revolution in France. The revolutionary movement
spread all over Europe, but Nicholas's first thought about the
concentration of counter-revolutionary forces for its suppression was limited immediately to the problem of "suppressing
the disturbance" in Poland, Galicia, and Poznan.

Prussia and Austria, Nicholas's former allies, were themselves shaken by the revolutionary movement. Prussia transformed itself and was drawn into the pan-German tendency.
"The Old Prussia no longer exists," wrote Nicholas. "It has
disappeared into Germany, and our venerable and close alliance has vanished with it." It had to be recognized that a reaction like that of the "era of Congresses" was impossible;
all that remained was to support partial intervention in German and Austrian affairs. In reality, the reactionary order
practiced in Russia remained confined within the national frontiers of that country.

Nicholas undoubtedly suffered a moment of fear that the
revolutionary tide might capture even his empire. Along with
an intensification of police terror he turned, as in 1826, to the
nobility with an appeal to assist the government in the preservation of "order" and with a declaration that the privileges of
landowners were sacred and inviolable. It seemed that an international conflict was imminent, one that was prepared to
incite revolutionary Europe against the Eastern autocrat.

Emperor Nicholas personally wrote the well-known manifesto of 14(26) March 1848, in which he spoke of the "new
disturbances" which had troubled Western Europe after "many
years of peace," and of the "mutiny and anarchy" which had
arisen in France but had enveloped Germany and was threatening Russia. Nicholas called on all Russians to defend "the
inviolability of the borders" of the empire, summoned them
to a struggle "for faith, tsar, and fatherland," and to a victory
which would give them the right to proclaim: "God is with
us, understand that and submit yourselves, people, for God is
with us." From then on, Nicholas loved to repeat this declaration on any occasion.

The manifesto also was published in German in Berlin
newspapers and signaled a direct challenge by the Russian autocrat to the revolutionary movement of the West. Nesselrode
even had to explain, in a diplomatic circular note, that this
manifesto did not at all signify any sort of aggressive intention
on Russia's part. "Let the nations of the West seek good for-
tune in revolutions," it was stated in this note. "Russia looks
calmly upon these movements, she does not participate in
them and will not oppose them; she does not envy the fate of
these nations even if they emerge from the turmoils of anarchy
and disorder toward a better future. Calmly Russia awaits the
further development of her own social relationships, resulting
from the passage of time and the wise solicitude of her tsar."
Conservative Russia placed itself in sharp opposition to revolutionary Europe. Nicholas stood before the West as the protect-
or and supporter of conservatism and reaction. And the vast
country subject to his rule seemed mute, submissive, and se-
curely isolated in its own traditions of the heavy authority of
the northern autocrat. The seething political life of the West
died down at the Russian frontier. To the poet who praised
Nicholas's regime, Russia was serene and haughty, an immov-
able and immutable gigantic cliff, about which crashed the
turbulent revolutionary waves of the western sea.*

*Tiutchev, *More i utes* [The Sea and the Cliff] , 1848. – *Author's Note*

In the ideology of the era of Nicholas I, Russia and Europe were in opposition to one another as two cultural and historical worlds of different sorts, which could not be compared in either the past, the present, or the future. The political reality reflected in such views was the increasing isolation of Russia within the framework of European international relations. With false confidence in its own strength, the Russia of Nicholas I placed itself and its interests in opposition to the entire European political world, on the ground of the Eastern Question. The ripening and increasing conflict broke out concerning the contest for mastery in the Near East, led to the destruction of the whole Nicholaevan political order, and even ruined the personal life of Nicholas I.

CHAPTER VI

THE INEVITABLE CATASTROPHE

The international successes of
Nicholas's policies at the end of
the 1840's were significant: the
unification of Germany had been
prevented; the Hungarian revolu-
tion had been crushed; Poland, dreaming of a new sovereignty,
had been suppressed. Following a renewal of revolution, France
seemed weakened. Ardently Nicholas welcomed the cruel suppression by General Cavaignac of the revolt of the Parisian pro-
letariat in the bloody June Days of 1848, and he perceived in
the bourgeois republic a conservative and counter-revolutionary force.

Russian diplomacy was even prepared for a rapproche-
ment with the French Republic in the event that it was not
possible to prevent the unification of Germany as a "mighty
and cohesive power unforeseen by existing treaties, and representative of 45 million people obedient to a unified, centralized authority, which would destroy any sort of equilibrium."
However, formal recognition of the Republic was delayed by
the rise of Louis Napoleon. He was seen, just as he himself
wished, as the restorer of the traditions of Napoleon I, and his
rise to power was viewed as a return to that regime which had
been vanquished by the forces of the coalition of all powers in
1813. Nonetheless, Nicholas reconciled himself to the selection of Louis Napoleon as president of the Republic and was
prepared for good relations with him, so long as he "remained

within the limits of his "present authority" and did not seek
to resurrect the Empire.

The Russian autocrat was attracted by the energy of Bona-
parte, in which he saw a force capable of restraining the revolutionary movement in France. But he tried to oppose the
transformation of the pretender into the Emperor Napoleon III,
and was particularly displeased by the "III," insisting that Europe knew of no Napoleon II. Before him loomed the spectre
of a renascent Napoleonic imperialism, destructive of the entire
system of "equilibrium," fundamentally opposed to the principle of "legitimacy," according to which there could be only
one dynasty in France — the Bourbons. Besides, any government born of revolution seemed unstable and flimsy, and thus
could not be accepted as an equal member in the "European
concert" of powers, not only as a matter of principle, but even
on practical grounds. Yet Nicholas's administration greatly
exaggerated these considerations, and for too long underrated
the results of the revolution which had abolished the Republic
in favor of the Empire of Napoleon III. Of course, it was
necessary to recognize him, following the example of all of
the powers. Nicholas merely twitted Napoleon III, and amused
himself, by refusing to call him the "brother" of his own autocracy and by calling him the "friend" or "cousin" instead.
Faulty vision increasingly concealed from him the true meaning of actual relationships.

This true meaning was to be found in the growing isolation of Russia. The old allies, Austria and Prussia, felt burdened by the heavy pressure of their neighbor hanging over
them. The powers furthest to the west, France and England,
were definitely hostile and extremely suspicious toward Russia.
Wrapped up in itself and placing itself resolutely in opposition
to Western Europe, Nicholaevan Russia all the more persistently
displayed its own special imperialism in the East.

Despite the obsolescence of its prejudices about the "old
order," France under Napoleon III taught an essential lesson
to Nicholas and the Russian bureaucracy. The more clearly the

Napoleonic political system revealed itself, the more a sympathy for it developed on the part of the Russian autocrat. In St. Petersburg one could not help but accept that he would "destroy demagogy," abolish "the parliamentary regime," and render "all of Europe a great service" by transforming France, this "hotbed of trouble and revolution," into a country disciplined by militarism and a police regime. But at the same time, disavowing the vestiges of feudal reaction which had destroyed the Bourbons, he took the path of serving the interests of the bourgeoisie by developing commercial and industrial capitalism. The Napoleonic regime presented the image of a bourgeois monarchy, shunning political freedom, with broad development of trade, industry, and education under the strict guardianship of a police state; it embodied that type of bureaucratic monarchy which henceforth became the ideal of the Russian bureaucracy. In this regime were resolved, apparently, those contradictions which so complicated the domestic policies of Nicholas and resulted in fruitless and deathly stagnation. The flowering of industrial capitalism in France proved to be consistent with the preservation of a bureaucratically organized autocracy.

But within Russia, the internal relations of the country would not permit such an evolution, without the abolition of serfdom. The zealous protection of industry was undermined by the weakness of the domestic market associated with serfdom. Not because of the satiation of demand but because of the weakness of consumption, pre-reform Russian imperialism launched a search for foreign markets in which to sell the products of developing Russian industry. Instead of expanding the base of national economic development by liberating the laboring classes from the ways of an obsolete system, Russian policy chose to expand this base abroad, in the Middle and Near East.

The defender of "equilibrium" in the West, from the very beginning of his reign Nicholas carried out an energetic

Eastern policy. The Persian and Turkish wars of the 1820s, the conquest of the Caucasus in a long-lasting struggle in the mountains, and the advance into Central Asia from the 18-30s on, were all parts of the program of this Eastern imperialism. It placed Russian interests in sharp opposition to the aspirations of England, and later also of France, for economic hegemony in Asia. At the same time, Russia — becoming England's rival in Persia and Central Asia — to a large degree was freed from the former predominance of England in her own demand for foreign trade both because of the development of overland trade with continental countries and, especially, because of her own protective tariffs. Only recently exploited like a colony herself, the country now not only achieved a certain industrial self-sufficiency but even entered into a rivalry which evoked great concern in England. All these questions and relations provided the conditions for a significant aggravation of international conflicts in the Near East. Here Nicholas's government consistently pursued the goal of Russian predominance, treating Turkey like a non-European country which lay outside the "European concert" and insisting on Russia's right to settle her own account with Turkey, uninfluenced by the Western powers.

Russia's advance in the Near East increased with the development of colonization in southern Russia, with the economic rise of New Russia and the entire Ukraine, and with the growth in the significance of the Black Sea trade routes. Already under Alexander I, the plan for the seizure of Moldavia and Wallachia had seemed close to realization. Russia's protection of the Balkan Slavs was strengthened in a series of treaties between the Emperor and the Sultan. The Danubian Principalities were governed by an "organic statute," granted under Russian pressure. An "organic statute" of the same origin was also received by Serbia in 1838. This term, which was used to signify the Balkan constitutions, was not without importance and was by no means accidental. An "organic statute" also had been substituted by Nicholas for the Polish Constitution, upon the suppression of the Polish revolt. The meaning of the constituent acts granted by the supreme authority, the "statutory charters" (as the term was translated in the Russian language), was that they were granted by the will of the sovereign. The Russian protectorate over the Danubian countries, which competed with the Sultan's authority over them, expressed itself in the guarantee of their systems, in the submission of their rulers to Russian influence, and in constant Russian intervention in their affairs. The weakening of the authority of the Ottoman Porte over regions subject to it seemed to Nicholas a sign of the imminent collapse of Turkey. Foreseeing what he believed to be the inevitable death of the "Sick Man," Nicholas strengthened his own position with regard to the legacy which would become available. He was certain that an arrangement could be made with England. It would be enough in Central Asia to delimit spheres of influence, to support the balance of power, and to preserve tranquility "in the buffer states which separated Russian domains from those of Great Britain," and to compete in the field of industry but not to enter into a conflict over political influence, and thus avoid a collision of the two great powers. As so often was the case with Nicholas in critical political questions, he proposed, insofar as possible, to avoid the consequences while tolerating their cause. And, in this case, he underrated the warning of wise old Wellington concerning advances into Asian countries: "In such undertakings, always remember that it is easy to go forward but difficult to come to a stop." The more far-sighted English sounded the alarm over the Russian menace which, with the appearance of Russians in Central Asia, threatened their possessions in India.

Concerning Near Eastern affairs, the plans and hopes of Nicholas's government vacillated between the urge to preserve a weak Turkey, which would be submissive to Russian pressure, and the expectation of the disintegration and partition

of Turkish territory. When the revolt of Mehmet-Ali[1] threatened a rebirth of Muslim power under Arab leadership, the
Russian army defended the Sultan and supported the shaky
Porte at the price of a treaty which enhanced Russian influence in the Near East. Twice, however, in 1844 during
a visit to London and in 1853 in a conversation with the
English envoy in St. Petersburg,[2] Nicholas personally discussed with English statesmen the possibility of partitioning
Turkey. He seriously thought that this question had come
to a head and that it was necessary to prepare for the moment of its unavoidable resolution. In London these revela-
tions by the Russian autocrat were taken as evidence of the
breadth of his aggressive plans, and the British answered
evasively but became ever more alert to the dangers posed by
Russian policy. Tenaciously, step by step, the English government gained from Nicholas an acknowledgement that Balkan affairs were not a problem peculiar to the Russian Empire, but a general question for the European powers, in which
neither one nor another of them should act without the agreement of the others.

Nicholas not only went along with these "conventions,"
by which English politicians tried to prevent arbitrary action
on his part in the East, but he himself also sought a rap-
prochement with England, in order to upset the Anglo-French
agreement. England, transformed by the parliamentary reform
of 1832 into a country entirely dominated by commercial and
industrial interests, followed with growing anxiety the course
of Nicholas's Eastern policy, the measures for the development of the Russian fleet, the control exercised by Russia
over the Danubian river route, the transformation of the Black
Sea into a sphere of Russian influence, and the conversion of
the Straits into an exit protected by the Turks under treaty
obligations[3] which gave Russia a path to world trade.

Greece served as the base of English influence in the
Near East, in opposition to Russia. With English support,
Greece had independently gained her political existence, and

DROJKI DE PLACE.

the naval and financial power of England placed the young
country under the powerful patronage of the "sovereign of
the seas." Here the roles were reversed. Russia and France
participated in the Grecophile policy of the English government, in order to limit the role of England in determining
the outcome of the struggle in the Balkans. Nicholas made
the independence of Greece part of the program of his own
policies, although he did not stop repeating that he regarded
the Greeks as "mutineers" against the legal authority of the
Sultan who were undeserving of either trust or sympathy.
This difference in attitude toward the Greeks and toward the
Danubian lands was characteristic. Nicholas recognized the
latter as essentially independent states under his protection,
but the Greek movement he evaluated in the old way, from
the point of view of legitimism, and he took it under his
wardship only as a counterweight to Anglo-French policy.

Such a complex web of relations in the Near East must
lead with fatal inevitability to a sharp and decisive conflict.
Yet Nicholas failed to perceive this. It is true that from the
1830s he discussed the possibility of a collision with England.
He tried to develop both his naval and land forces, when
technical means and economic power clearly were inadequate.
But to the very end he hoped to avoid this collision. For a
long time he deceived himself by counting on an agreement
between Russia and England on all matters of Eastern politics, both in Central Asia and in the Balkan peninsula, which
would reconcile their antagonism and would foreshadow the
decline or even the destruction of the Anglo-French alliance.
the active efforts of Russian diplomacy at the end of the
1840s and beginning of the 1850s, which Nicholas himself
directed, were permeated by a yearning to strengthen the
disintegrating system of peaceful relations and to extricate
Russia from her growing isolation, by using methods which
were already inadequate and were divorced from political
reality.

Nicholas, living in a world of "dynastic mythology," according to the phrase of his German biographer,* ascribed decisive significance in the course of political events to the personal relations, views, and assumptions of those who ruled. He sometimes confused the meaning of formal international obligations and the personal conversations or correspondence which were exchanged by the leading powers. The techniques of international relations he conceived as personal dealings and relations between sovereigns, either directly or through envoys empowered by them. The dependence of policy upon the conflict of parliamentary parties and changes in constitutional states, in his opinion, deprived it of stability and deprived the treaties of such states of lasting significance. He based his essential conclusions and calculations upon Prussian friendship, upon Austrian gratitude for the joint action against the Hungarians, upon English prudence, to which he referred in his personal negotiations, upon his misunderstanding of the self-esteem of Napoleon III, whom it was necessary to flatter by an invitation to St. Petersburg with the promise of a "fraternal" welcome by the Russian autocrat (which the French emperor naturally took as an offensive lack of tact), and the like. Exaggerating the importance of the methods which were traditional in international relations in the era of absolutism, Nicholas dispelled, with his diplomatic illusions, any possible expectation of an inevitable eruption of a major conflict. In this lay one of the roots of the unique tragedy of that position in which he found himself at the start of the Crimean War. Another was the dissolution, out of what was revealed as horrifying weakness, of the bulky state apparatus before the problems of a strenuous military test.

Official phraseology (rather than ideology) connected even the Balkan policy of Nicholas I with ancient Russian

*Theodor Schiemann, *Geschichte Russlands unter Kaiser Nikolaus I.* 4 vols., Berlin, 1908-1919. — *Author's Note*

traditions. Miscalculating that the Western powers would, after all, yield and not enter into a decisive contest against the
Russian protectorate over Turkey and her Christian subjects,
Nicholas put point blank the question of his claim to exercise a genuine right of protection of the Orthodox Church
within the borders of the Turkish Empire, that is, in the form
of the legal and administrative significance of the Patriarch of
Constantinople over all the Orthodox populations of the Ottoman Porte. And to the Turkish declaration of war on October 19, 1854, he responded with a manifesto in which the
cause of the war was established as the protection of the legal right of Russia to defend the Orthodox faith in the East.

This policy — a direct challenge to the Western powers
— resulted in an impossible struggle without allies against
the entire coalition. Technical backwardness made the role
of the Russian navy insignificant in this conflict; the mori-
bund rigidity of Nicholas's system and the habits of irres-
ponsible routine weakened the Russian army. With its strict
military bearing, this army turned out to be too passive an
instrument of the higher command. Severe and callous drill
undermined the energy and resourcefulness of its individual
tactical units, and the habit of mechanically arranged movement of solid masses, worked out on the parade grounds,
was quite useless on the field of battle. The vivid and complete enthusiasm of the army of 1812 did not have the sympathy of Nicholas and his brothers. In their conviction, the
campaigns of 1812-14 corrupted the army and destroyed
discipline; every energy was directed to eliminate that spirit,
which was deemed too civilian. But the extreme disorgani-
zation of the home front ever more heavily weighed upon
the course of the war, in its inability to supply the army and
in its medical and commissary aspects. Both the outward and
internal conditions in which the war was waged were utterly
destructive of Nicholas's political system.

At the end of 1854 a pathetic manifesto was helplessly
and vainly issued, in which Nicholas tried to make the war

seem "patriotic," like that of 1812, calling on the country
to defend itself, and on February 18, 1855, he died, so unexpectedly and in such a depressed frame of mind that many
did not want to believe it was a natural death.

CHAPTER VII

OBSERVATIONS

It was said of the youngest of Paul's sons, Michael, that while abroad in civilian clothing he was a very simple and affable person with those with whom he conversed, but that when he returned to Russia he changed his clothes at the border for a tightly-fitting military dress-coat, spoke to his reflection in the mirror before which he was arranging himself, and said "Goodby, Michael Pavlovich," and once again presented that harsh and rigid front by which he was known in Russia. That same duality which concealed a conventional personal human nature and, ultimately, inevitably distorted it, was also characteristic of his brothers, Constantine and Nicholas. A severe, unbalanced disposition, petty formalism, and fits of gruff temper were common to Constantine and Michael. Of course, such traits could be attributed to a great extent to their legacy from their father. But the whole mode of life, in the militaristic atmosphere which prevailed, created the conditions for the extreme development of these traits.

Nicholas knew the peculiarities of his brothers and often felt burdened by them, but nothing could be done about it. His relations with his elder brother, Constantine, were complicated by those rights to the throne which were passed from him to Nicholas, the memory of which was preserved in Constantine's lifelong title of Crown Prince, but he never once tried to assert his authority as the elder brother to the trustee of the legacies of Alexander I. Yet despite this, the

dynastic outlook of Nicholas endowed his relations with his
brothers with a special character: he could not deny them
their right to some participation in the exercise of authority,
at least in military command. In his letters to his wife he
sometimes complained of the harsh disposition of Michael,
whose escapades made an undesirable impression upon both
society and the army. He considered Michael neurotic. "It
is lamentable," wrote Nicholas, "but there is nothing I can
do. In fifty years he could not be cured of such neurosis."

Nicholas was, in general, more balanced than his brothers, but even his nature was not free of those same traits,
which sometimes were revealed quite sharply. And he easily
lost his self-control in irritation, and then let fly rough
threats or arbitrary punishments; he lost himself in despair
over failure, and then cravenly complained and even cried.
He did not have a strong, monolithic nature, although it is
understandable why he was often depicted that way. His
image, as emperor, seemed monolithic in outlook and political conduct because he consistently adhered to a definite
style of the autocratic genre. This was not a matter of
character, however, but an historical role, and it did not
come easily to him.

In 1847 Bakunin[1] characterized the internal state of
Russia in this way: "The domestic affairs of the country
are going extremely badly. There is complete anarchy under
the label of order. The facade of bureaucratic formalism
conceals terrible wounds; our administrative, judicial, and
financial systems are all a lie — a lie to deceive foreign opinion, a lie to lull the conscience of the sovereign, who all the
more willingly lends himself to it because the real state of
things scares him." Nicholas struck him as a foreigner in Russia; he was "a sovereign of German origins who never understood either the needs or the character of the Russian people."

And in 1858, after Nicholas's death, the direct opposite
of Bakunin, Valuev,[2] commenced his brilliant bureaucratic
career with a memorandum, "Thoughts of a Russian," wherein

he ascribed the chief cause of the fall of Sevastopol[3] to "general, official falsehood." Such was the almost universal judgment concerning Nicholaevan Russia.

The head of this official Russia loved adornment and gave his performance theatrical effects. Outbursts of unrestrained abruptness were concealed behind the facade of generosity. Nicholas was able, after a rude insult delivered publically, to solemnly put on an act of asking forgiveness, and he thought that one made up for the other, knowing that such gestures would produce an impression on those who were steeped in the awareness of the inequality of master and servant. Foreigners, not without irony and indignation, noted this mixture of harsh arrogance and vulgar popularity-seeking in his conduct: humble servants had to tremble before their masters and to measure in gold their greeting, handshake, kiss.

The very "nationalism" which formed one of the foundations of official doctrine degenerated into a decorative masquerade ball of Russian national costumes at court festivals. This masquerade sometimes took on a cruel political significance, as when, for example, in Warsaw it was prescribed that Polish noblewomen should present themselves to the empress in the traditional Russian sarafans. The Poles obeyed, and Nicholas wrote with pleasure: "So my goal was attained; they wear not Polish, but Russian costume." Bakunin was correct: genuine Russian self-esteem would have shown Nicholas that such a scene humiliated not the Poles, but the Russian sarafan. To Nicholas such feelings were alien.

Indeed, even his beloved military cause degenerated into mere display, which was injurious to military technology and agonizing for the army. There was a patriot who decided to explain to him that the methods he had adopted for training the troops would lead to "the destruction of the physical powers of the army" and to an unusual increase in the number of deaths, injuries, and disabilities. "The method

of training adopted," he wrote, "is destructive of human
life. A soldier is pulled upwards and downwards simultane-
ously, upwards to reach a certain height, downwards to
stretch his legs and toes. A soldier must, with his every
muscle and nerve, slowly stretch out his leg straight in front
of him and then quickly lower it, putting his entire body
into it. All of this stretching and shaking is injurious to his
internal organs; after all of these exertions, repeated several
times a day for two hours at a time, the soldier goes back to
the barracks like a horse who has been beaten on his legs."
But the results of this mass torture — the harmonious movement of large numbers of men in colorful uniforms at inspections and parades — delighted Nicholas with its brilliant
pictorial quality. Here he found the highest embodiment of
"order." His aesthetics were steeped in militarism, as its
finest embodiment. His politics and aesthetics were remarkably in harmony with each other: at strict attention! He
loved uniformity, regularity, absolute symmetry, and per-
fection of form.

The classicism in architecture which had been inherited
Nicholas's aesthetics had an effect upon the construction of buildings during his era. It was of personal interest
to him and, besides that, he indeed regarded it as his obligation to scrutinize everything and to decide everything himself, not only in matters of state but even, for example, in
questions of art. In the study which A.N. Benois[4] devoted
to this activity of Nicholas, some curious observations are
brought together. Not a single private home in the center
of St. Petersburg, nor a single public building in Russia, was
erected without his knowledge. He examined all proposals
for such buildings, gave his own instructions, and approved
them personally.

The classicism in architecture which had been inherited
by the Nicholaevan epoch gradually withered in the new atmosphere, took on more rigid forms, and was subjected to
"barracks-like" regularity. In approaching any problem,
Nicholas became petty, making inquiries about "elegant" and

"cozy" little nooks. But even this "Nicholaevan classicism" was not characteristic of the age. Inherently contradictory in its entire way of life and its entire structure, the era of Nicholas I got rid of old forms and vainly searched for new ones, often falling into an eclecticism which combined heterogeneous styles. And Nicholas himself, beginning in the 1830s, was captivated by "all that which was enthralling in the courts of Frederick William IV of Prussia, Ludwig and Maximilian I of Bavaria, and even the despised Louis-Philippe." Artistic work was pervaded by a "certain chaotic quality and by that mixture of styles which destroys the impression it gives." Any impression of a common, integrated style vanished.

In the spirit of the times, study of and interest in authentic Russian antiquity began. But its forms were adopted, also in the spirit of the times, with all the conventions of "official nationality." For example, there was a characteristic introduction into the "Empire style" of such ornamental features as the two-headed eagle, on the one hand, and, on the other, of ancient Slavic weapons instead of Roman ones, or the arid and barren attempts to introduce a "national" element into the style of construction of both secular buildings and churches. "In official buildings," Benois noted, "dryness, severity, and coldness were expressed, of course, whether it was still done in the classical style or in the new spirit with the intention of communicating 'nationalism,' such as in palaces (the Nicholas Palace and Great Palace in the Moscow Kremlin), in the Orthodox churches of K.A. Thon[5] numerous noble assembly buildings, provincial houses, offices, barracks, hospitals, and similar buildings, not unjustly labelled by the term 'in the barracks style.'"

As throughout the regime, official conventions determined and affected creative work. Nicholas himself, in his personal experiences, was typical of his era. He sometimes felt keenly the crushing pressure of his role. Here are characteristic lines from one of his letters:

My fate is strange; they tell me that I am one of
the most powerful rulers in the world, and it must
be said that anything — that is, anything permissible — is possible for me, that I could perhaps,
at my discretion, be anywhere and do anything
I wished. In fact, however, in my case it is just
the opposite. And if I were asked about the
cause of this anomaly, there is only one answer:
duty! Yes, this is not an empty word for one
who since youth has been taught to understand
it, as I have. This word has a sacred meaning,
before which all personal motives must give way,
all must fall silent before this one feeling and
yield to it, until you disappear in the grave.
Such is my watchword. It is hard, I admit; it
is more agonizing to me than I can express, but
I was born to be unhappy.

Another time Nicholas complained about the impossibility of fulfilling his obligations and about his excessively
strenuous activity: parade-watches, inspections of the fleet,
manoeuvers, artillery tests, the unsuccessful course of the
Caucasian campaigns, the work of the commissions on pea
sant affairs, the recurrent question of railroad construction,
and so on — he had to concern himself with all of them and
to hurry everywhere. His feeling of depression was obvious.
It was sustained by his awareness of the impossibility of
correcting the rampant embezzlement and abuses and of the
fruitless waste of effort and money. "I work," he wrote to
Frederick William, "in order to numb myself, but my heart
will be strained as long as I live." He withdrew into himself, became ever more sharp and temperamental; his internal tension and confusion were expressed in outbursts of temper and in his rigid, cold, self-control. "It is sometimes terrible to see," wrote the observant Countess Nesselrode,
"what a hard expression the Emperor has on his face; and he

makes sudden decisions and acts with incomprehensible haste."
The emperor was regarded as inclined to melancholy and
hypochondria. This mood appeared early and showed itself
clearly by the beginning of the 1840s, a long time before the
obvious and frightening signs of the dangerous crisis in the
domestic forces of the country. The inevitable bankruptcy
of the "system" already made itself felt then. The same
Countess Nesselrode wrote in 1842: "It is astonishing how
the machine continues to run. A dull sorrow reigns everywhere, everyone anticipates and fears the dangers which may
arrive without warning instead of threatening us." This un-
clear, undefined fear kept the ruling circles, headed by the
emperor, unders a constant strain. It could not be removed,
but was suppressed by severe despotism and concealed by a
display of official well-being and order. The longer Nicholas
supported the shaky edifice of the entire government, the
less he believed in his strength.

Of course, the emperor steadfastly played his role in his
own way. But it often seemed beyond his power. Even all
the outward conditions of imperial life which he cultivated
with such apparent enthusiasm often tired him. It was noted
that in the absence of the empress he lived far more simply,
refusing many comforts. To him, the barracks were dearer
than the palace, and in the palace he took shelter in the
cramped rooms of the lower floor with its more modest
furniture.

A.N. Benois recorded a characteristic feature of the emperor's building projects. "The split personality of Nicholas
Pavlovich," wrote Benois, "as a man and as Emperor, was also
reflected in the buildings he erected: in all the edifices which
were meant for himself or his family, there is evident a desire
for intimacy, coziness, comfort, and simplicity."

The desire for a personal life for himself divided the emperor's frame of mind. He was regarded as a good family man,
and he maintained the tone of an attentive and loving spouse
in his relations with the empress. But all the conditions of

his life and, on top of this, the sickliness of his wife, were
not slow to destroy the idyll of family life, to connect it
with the idea of "duty," and to give it a pretentious character. Nicholas struggled for a long time with his attraction
to the lady-in-waiting Barbara Nelidova, but he ended by
establishing a second family. The position of Kleinmichael[6]
as an influential favorite was supported by the fact that he
adopted the children from this imperial liaison.

Both in Nicholas's personal and official lives there were
many breaches which became increasingly wide. His personal
life was distorted and stifled by the conditions of being emperor; his official life by the conditions of the historical moment. Imperial power fostered the brilliant illusion of omnipotence, but at the cost of a break with the vital forces of
the country and the suppression of its urgent, pressing needs.
The energies of the state, paralyzed by a cowardly conservatism and fearful of shocks, were directed aggressively toward
struggle beyond Russia's frontiers. This struggle possessed
dual foundations. It was conducted both for the protection,
on a general European scale, of the ancient principles of the
political order, the destruction of which would undermine
the position of the autocratic Russian Empire, and for the
conquest by Russia of a possibly significant place on the
routes of international trade.

Nicholaevan Russia did not withstand the test of this
struggle. Russia's power proved to be imaginary: the Northern Colossus stood on feet of clay. In its entirety the political system of Nicholas I was destroyed. And his own life
was cut short. He died with the awareness that he was leaving his son a grave legacy, that thirty years of governmental
had ended in catastrophe. The war destroyed the ornamental trappings of official Russia. Wrote a contemporary: "It
opened our eyes and made us see things as they really were:
the boon which thirty years of peace and tranquility had
provided us did not exist." And yet another contemporary
voice, which was raised under the fresh impression of the

emperor's death: "I never doubted that he would not endure this. Many things, and one can say most of all this unfortunate war, hastened the destruction of the mighty organism and led to the death of a man who recognized his many errors. To a man such as he was, there remained only this choice: abdication or death."

An abdication was unthinkable to Nicholas. There remained death. And, on February 18, 1855, death freed him from the summing-up of the results of his whole life. Rumors were heard that he had poisoned himself. It seemed probable. This was hurriedly refuted. Already on March 24, the Second Section of His Majesty's Own Chancery published "The Last Hours of the Life of Emperor Nicholas I" in four languages (Russian, French, English, and Polish), and even earlier, on March 3, a brochure had been published semi-officially in Brussels on the same subject by Poggenpohl.[7] But the question of Nicholas's death did not subside, and a recent, thoroughly executed examination of all the facts for and against his suicide leads to the conclusion that this question cannot be considered settled.[8] Whereas the German biographer of Nicholas I, Theodor Schiemann, firmly denies such a possibility, based, however, only on the idea that suicide would have been too contradictory to the religious convictions of Nicholas, N.S. Shtakelberg concludes his study with the acknowledgement that it was psychologically possible and cannot, on the evidence of the sources, be either proved or disproved.

NOTES

1. Quoted from N.K. Shilder (or Schilder), *Imperator Nikolai Pervyi, ego zhizn i tsarstvovanie* (St. Petersburg, 1903), Volume I, p. 147.

2. T. Schiemann, *Geschichte Russlands unter Kaiser Nikolaus I* (Berlin, 1904-1919), Volume II, p. XII.

3. Quoted from *Sbornik Imperatorskogo Russkogo Istoricheskogo Obshchestva,* Volume XCVIII, p. 36. Italics in the original.

4. From a letter to Frederick William IV of Prussia, of August 26, 1854, published as an appendix to Schiemann's study: T. Schiemann, *op. cit.,* Volume IV, pp. 434-435.

5. In a letter to Prince Michael Gorchakov, the commander in the Crimea, quoted in M.A. Polievktov, *Nikolai I. Biografiia i obzor tsarstvovaniia* (Moscow, 1918), p. 376.

6. *Ibid.*

7. S.S. Uvarov, "Tsirkuliarnoe predlozhenie G. Upravliaiushchego Ministerstvom Narodnogo Prosveshcheniia Nachalstvam Uchebnykh Okrugov 'O vstuplenii v upravlenie Ministerstvom'," *Zhurnal Ministerstva Narodnogo Prosveshcheniia,* 1834, Part I, p. 1. For a full treatment of Official Nationality see my study: N. Riasanovsky, *Nicholas I and Official Nationality in Russia, 1825-1855,* Berkeley and Los Angeles, 1959.

8. S.S. Uvarov, *Desiatiletie ministerstva narodnogo prosveshcheniia, 1833-1843* (St. Petersburg, 1864), pp. 2-3. Emphasis in the original.

9. S.P. Shevyrev, "Vzgliad russkogo na sovremennoe obrazovanie Evropy," *Moskvitianin,* Part I, pp. 292-295.

10. S.P. Shevyrev, *Istoriia Imperatorskogo Moskovskogo Universiteta, napisannaia k stoletnemu ego iubileiu, 1755-1855* (Moscow, 1855), pp. 469-470.

11. F. I. Tiutchev, *Polnoe sobranie sochinenii* (St. Petersburg, 1913), p. 366.

12. *Svod Zakonov Rossiiskoi Imperii* (St. Petersburg, 1832), Volume I, Article 1.

13. Quoted in an appendix to Shilder, *op.cit.*, Volume I, p. 758.

14. S.S. Uvarov, *Essai sur les mysteres d'Eleusis* (Paris, 1816), p. 30.

15. M.P. Pogodin, *Prostaia rech o modrenykh veshchakh* (Moscow, 1875), p. 91.

16. N.P. Barsukov, *Zhizn i trudy M.P. Pogodina* (22 vols., St. Petersburg, 1888-1910), Volume II, p. 17.

17. N.I. Grech, *Zapiski o moei zhizni* (Moscow-Leningrad, 1930), p. 104.

18. *Ibid.*, p. 211.

19. F. V. Bulgarin, *Vospominaniia* (6 vols., St. Petersburg, 1846-1849), Volume I, pp. 14-15.

20. Richard Pipes, *Karamzin's Memoir on Ancient and Modern Russia: A Translation and Analysis* (New York, 1966), pp. 192-195.

21. Barsukov, *op. cit.*, Volume V, p. 22.

22. M.P. Pogodin, *Istoriko-politicheskie pisma i zapiski v prodolzhenii Krymskoi voiny. 1853-1856* (Moscow, 1874), p. 268. Except for "the system of publicity" which found no favor in the eyes of the emperor, Pogodin's statement represented faithfully the conviction of Nicholas I and of his associates.

23. M. P. Pogodin, *Rechi, proiznesennye v torzhestvennykh i prochikh sobraniiakh, 1830-1872* (Moscow, 1872), p. 90.

24. N.V. Gogol, *Sochineniia.* V. V. Kallash, ed. (10 vols., St. Petersburg, n.d.), Volume VIII, p. 163.

25. N. M. Karamzin, *Istoriia gosudarstva rossiiskogo.* Many editions.

26. S.S. Uvarov, *Desiatiletie ministerstva narodnogo prosveshcheniia, 1833-1843,* pp. 97-98. Ustrialov's discussion of the reign of Nicholas I was corrected by the emperor in person.

27. See especially Barsukov, *op. cit.*, Volume I, p. 56, p. 211; Volume II, p. 293. Shevyrev fell under the same spell as Pogodin. For instance, in 1829, at the age of twenty-three, he noted in his diary: "Each evening certainly, and sometimes in the mornings too, I assign it to myself as an unfailing duty to read the life of Peter the Great

and everything related to him." And he added the categorical imper-
ative: "Be such a man as Christ, be such a Russian as Peter the
Great." This account with its quotations is from: N. Ch., "Shevyrev, Stepan Petrovich," *Russkii biograficheskii slovar* (St. Petersburg,
1911), Volume "Shevanov" to "Shiutts," pp. 19-29. Quoted from
p. 22.

28. But apotheosis was not enough. Nicholas I read the play and
resolved: *"The person of Emperor Peter the Great must be for
every Russian an object of veneration and of love; to bring it onto
the stage would be almost sacrilege, and therefore entirely improper.
Prohibit the publication."* Barsukov, *op. cit.,* Volume IV, p. 13.
Italics in the original.

29. Bulgarin, *op. cit.,* Volume I, pp. 200-201.

30. Quoted in A. G. Dementev, *Ocherki po istorii russkoi zhurnal-
istiki 1840-1850 gg.* (Moscow-Leningrad, 1951), p. 185.

31. Pogodin, *Rechi, proiznesennye v torzhestvennykh i prochikh
sobraniiakh, 1830-1872,* pp. 39-40. As a young man Pogodin had
noted with pride that Russian soldiers away on a campaign preferred starvation to breaking a fast. Barsukov, *op. cit.,* Volume I,
p. 94.

32. Tiutchev, *op. cit.,* p. 344. Ustrialov, dutifully underlining all the
principles of Official Nationality, summarized the character of the Russian people as follows: "Profound and quiet piety, boundless devotion
to the throne, obedience to the authorities, remarkable patience, a lu-
cid and solid intelligence, a kind and hospitable soul, a gay temper,
courage amidst the greatest dangers, finally national pride which had
produced the conviction that there was no country in the world better than Russia, no ruler mightier than the Orthodox tsar." N.G. Ustrialov, *Russkaia istoriia.* Fifth edition (2 vols., St. Petersburg, 1855),
Volume II, p. 15.

33. Thus, beginning with the report for 1831, Russian replaced French
as the language of the annual reports of the Third Department of His
Majesty's Own Chancery, the gendarmerie, which Count Alexander
Benckendorff presented to the emperor. Nicholas I also sponsored
"nationality" by such means as the introduction of native Russian
dress for ladies at the court — to everyone's delight, or so wrote the
ubiquitous head of the gendarmerie: "On the sixth of December of

the past year of 1833, there appeared for the first time in the Palace our Ladies and the Empress Herself in national costume and in Russian headdress. The beauty of this garb aside, it evoked, because of the feeling of nationality, a general approval." ("Otchet III-go Otdeleniia Sobstvennoi Ego Imperatorskogo Velichestva Kantseliarii i Korpusa Zhandarmov za 1834-i god," TsGAOR, 109/85/2, quoted from pp. 3-4.)

Benckendorff's general judgment on the matter deserves attention: ". . . one can firmly state that no characteristic of the Reign of the present Sovereign obtained for Him so much love, so many praises, so much general approval as His constant effort, from the very first day of His Reign, to glorify everything Russian, to sponsor everything Native and gradually to extirpate the slavish imitation of foreigners." (*Ibid.*, p.3)

34. S.P. Shevyrev, "Vzgliad russkogo na sovremennoe obrazovanie Evropy," *Moskvitianin* (1841, Number 1), pp. 219-296. Quoted from p. 219.

35. Schiemann, *op. cit.*, Volume II, p. XII.

36. Quoted from I. M. Trotskii, *Trete otdelenie pri Nikolae I* (Moscow, 1930), pp. 34-35. Recently two books were published in English on the Third Department, the first stressing the general cultural setting and the second administration and functioning: Sidney Monas, *The Third Section: Police and Society in Russia under Nicholas I* (Cambridge, Mass., 1961) and P.S. Squire, *The Third Department: The Establishment and Practice of the Political Police in the Russia of Nicholas I* (Cambridge, 1968).

37. Trotskii, *op. cit.*, p. 111.

38. Shevyrev, *Istoriia Imperatorskogo Moskovskogo Universitets, napisannaia k stoletnemu ego iubileiu, 1755-1855,* p. 483.

39. This imperial comment is quoted from Paul Milioukov (Miliukov), Ch. Seignobos and L. Eisenmann, *Histoire de Russie* (3 vols., Paris, 1932-1933), Volume II, p. 785. For the context, see Barsukov (*op. cit.*, Volume X, pp. 525-538, especially p. 538).

40. *Sbornik Imperatorskogo Russkogo Istoricheskogo Obshchestva,* Volume XCVIII, p. 114-115. Italics in the original.

41. N.M. Druzhinin, *Gosudarstvennye krestiane i reforma P.D. Kiseleva.* 2 vols., Moscow-Leningrad, 1946-1958.

42. Nikitenko, *op. cit.,* Volume I, p. 441.

43. *Ibid.,* pp. 393-417; and M.O. Gershenzon, ed., *Epokha Nikolaia I* (Moscow, 1911), p. 105, *re* musical notations. Nikitenko himself served as a censor.

44. Pogodin, *Istoriko-politicheskie pisma i zapiski v prodolzhenii Krymskoi voiny, 1853-1856,* p. 259.

45. Shilder, *op. cit.,* Volume II, pp. 271-272.

46. Shilder, *op. cit.,* p. 390. Emphasis in the original.

NOTES TO THE TEXT

1. When Alexander I died in Taganrog without leaving an heir, it was assumed that his oldest brother, Constantine, would succeed him. However, in 1820 Constantine had entered into a morganatic marriage with a Polish Catholic countess. In a subsequent exchange of letters between Alexander and Constantine, the latter had renounced his rights to the crown, and in 1823 Alexander had signed a manifesto written by Metropolitan Filaret of Moscow which declared his next brother, Nicholas, to be the heir-apparent. (Nicholas had by this time produced a son, thus offering the hope of the continuation of the Romanov dynasty in the male line.) Strangely, Alexander did not publish the manifesto, but ordered sealed copies of it (and the exchange of letters with Constantine) to be deposited in the Moscow Uspensky Cathedral, the State Council, the Senate, and the Holy Synod, with the provision that they be opened upon his death. Nicholas himself knew of the manifesto and of Constantine's renunciation, yet when Alexander died he initially swore allegiance to Constantine and required others to do the same, probably because he knew of his own unpopularity and wished to pressure Constantine into making a *public* renunciation. For over two weeks there was a virtual interregnum, until at last December 14, 1825, was fixed as the date for taking a new oath to Emperor Nicholas I.

2. The *Pugachevshchina* was a large-scale peasant rebellion led by a Don Cossack, Emelian Ivanovich Pugachev, in 1773-1775. Pugachev's forces managed to capture Kazan, Saratov, Penza, and other important cities before the revolt was crushed and Pugachev himself executed in 1775. The rebellion served to remind the nobility of its own weakness and insecurity and of the need for a strong government able to protect it from the fury of the peasantry, and led Catherine II to enact provincial reforms to strengthen local administration, which had appeared helpless to deal with the revolt.

3. Prior to the reign of Peter the Great, succession to the throne had passed to the eldest son. In 1722, however, Peter issued a decree which proclaimed the emperor's right to appoint his own successor, ostensibly so that he might eliminate from the line of succession any member of the dynasty he deemed unfit to rule. This arbitrary power had contributed to the political instability of the Russian Empire in the eighteenth century. One of Paul's earliest legislative acts was the abolition of the right of the sovereign to name his own successor. The law promulgated in 1797, on the day of his own coronation, made the crown hereditary in the House of Romanov and defined the order of succession.

4. Of non-royal lineage and of Roman Catholic faith, her marriage to Constantine was declared morganatic. See footnote 1, above.

5. After the death of his first wife, in 1776, Paul married Sophie Dorothea, princess of Würtemberg, who assumed the name Maria Fedorovna upon her conversion to Russian Orthodoxy. She presided over a somewhat pretentious literary and artistic salon, staged theatricals, and played an active role in various philanthropic endeavors, especially as Dowager Empress. She died in 1828.

6. Nicholas's links with German nobles began in his childhood. His mother, Maria Fedorovna, was a German princess, and his father descended from the ruling houses of Holstein-Gottorp and Anhalt-Zerbst. In addition to his German relatives, he had been raised by such Baltic Germans as Countess Lieven (who supervised his care as a child). Prince Karl Lieven served Nicholas as Minister of Public Instruction from 1828 to 1833. Count Vladimir Adlerberg, another Baltic German who was Nicholas's childhood playmate and remained his close friend, later held the post of head of the imperial postal service.

7. General Matthew Lamsdorff (1745-1826), another Baltic German nobleman who had had a distinguished military and administrative career, was put in charge of Nicholas's education. He is generally acknowledged to have been a stern, rigid, and even cruel tutor.

8. An estate near St. Petersburg, formerly owned by one of Catherine the Great's lovers, Gregory Orlov, which she gave to Paul in 1783. Here Paul lived the life of a country gentleman and garrison commander from 1783 to 1796. Like Nicholas I himself, Paul had a passion for the army, and the Gatchina garrison, dressed in Prussian uniforms, was often drilled by Paul personally. Although Gatchina continued to serve as a country estate for the Romanovs, the name retained the connotation of harsh and rigid discipline.

9. Count Aleksei Andreevich Arakcheev (1769-1834) served as Paul's chief advisor at Gatchina and commanded the latter's private army there. A harsh disciplinarian, both publicly and privately, he became a central figure in the reign of Alexander I, serving variously as Minister of Defense and personal advisor. He is noted, too, for the system of "military colonies" which he established in the latter part of Alexander I's reign.

10. General Alexander Khristoforovich Benckendorff (1783-1844) served as first head of the Third Section and as Chief of Gendarmes.

11. The Decembrists comprised a movement largely composed of aristocratic officers who conducted an ill-organized and unsuccessful revolt in St. Petersburg in December, 1825. Their general goals were the overthrow of the existing government and the abolition of serfdom, but there was significant disagreement among the moderate and radical elements as to how these and other goals might best be implemented and what sort of political system should be established. Following the suppression of the revolt, five leaders of the movement were executed, and many others were exiled to Siberia or received other punishments. Often called "the first Russian revolutionaries," they inspired subsequent generations of liberals and radicals. To both their admirers and critics, and especially to Nicholas himself, they were particularly significant because of their elevated social origins: the banner of revolution had been raised not by the oppressed, but by the most privileged members of Russian society, who put their own self-interest aside in the name of the common good.

12. Well-known scholars, Michael Andreevich Balugiansky and Hein-rich Storch presided over Nicholas's "advanced" education, in such subjects as political economy, logic, moral philosophy, natural law, and the history of law, mathematics and science, and ancient and modern languages. Balugiansky later served as assistant to Speransky in the codification of Russian laws in the 1830s.

13. Nestor V. Kukolnik served as one of Nicholas's tutors. A third-rate playwright, his pompous and patriotic works (such as "The Hand of the Almighty Saved the Fatherland") appealed to Nicholas. Indeed, an unfavorable review of that play by Nicholas Polevoi in the *Moscow Telegraph* resulted in the closing down of that journal.

14. As a young officer, Yakov Ivanovich Rostovtsev had been unsuc-cessfully recruited by a leader of one of the Decembrist organizations and had reported the existence of a conspiracy to Nicholas. A lead-ing ideologist in Nicholas's reign, he rose to the rank of general and later served Alexander II as Chairman of the Editing Commission which drafted the statutes emancipating Russia's serfs.

CHAPTER II

1. Nicholas Mikhailovich Karamzin (1766-1826) was an eminent historian and belle-lettrist, a leading representative of the Sentiment-al school in Russian literature, and an important figure in the de-velopment of the modern Russian literary language. His monument-al *History of the Russian State* (12 vols.) was pervaded by his ad-miration of autocracy and his defense of serfdom. His *Memoir on Ancient and Modern Russia* (translated and edited by Richard N. Pipes: Cambridge, Mass., 1959), written in 1811, contained his re-flections on the contemporary state of Russia in the light of his in-terpretation of Russian history. A strongly-worded attack upon the governmental reforms then championed by Alexander I's close ad-visor, M.M. Speransky, and an eloquent statement of the mutual in-terests of the autocracy and the nobility, the *Memoir* remained a classic expression of conservative thought and, as such, exerted con-siderable influence upon the ideology of Nicholaevan Russia.

2. The Treaty of Tilsit, signed by Alexander I and Napoleon in 1807, not only ended the war between Russia and France, but provided for an alliance, albeit an uneasy one, between the two powers. Although it bought time for Russia to prepare for the final conflict with revolutionary France which erupted in 1812, the treaty was extremely unpopular in Russia, for both economic and ideological reasons.

3. Alexander Aleksandrovich Bestuzhev (1797-1837), the scion of a prominent Russian family, served as an army officer, was an active contributor to various periodical journals, and was a member of the Decembrist group known as the Northern Society. Following the unsuccessful Decembrist coup, he gave himself up to the authorities and confessed his part in the conspiracy. Under the pen-name of Marlinsky he wrote a number of poems and novels, many of which dealt with his post-1826 observations during his exile in the Caucasus.

4. Prince Victor Pavlovich Kochubei (1768-1834) was an intimate associate of Alexander I, a member of his "Unofficial Committee" of advisors, and one of the most prominent statesmen of the first quarter of the nineteenth century. Among his various governmental posts were those of Minister of the Interior (1802-1807, 1819-1823), President of the State Council (1827-1834), and Chairman of the Committee of Ministers (1827-1834).

CHAPTER III

1. Of the two types of obligation owed by Russia's vast serf population, *obrok* consisted of a monetary payment or payment in kind, while *barshchina* was a labor service of a specified amount. In general, *barshchina* was the prevalent form of obligation in the black-soil regions, with *obrok* being more common in the less fertile regions. It is generally felt that *barshchina* was the more onerous burden. In the nineteenth century, the norm for *barshchina* was fixed at three days per week, but this maximum was often disregarded.

2. In 1775, following the suppression of the Pugachev rebellion, Catherine II enacted a provincial reform which was aimed at decentralizing administration, to permit local authorities to respond more

quickly to local problems. The number of provinces in the Russian Empire was increased and each was headed by a civil governor or governor-general who was responsible to the central government. Within each province, lines of authority and spheres of jurisdiction were more clearly defined.

3. Vissarion Grigorevich Belinsky (1811-1848) was a leading Russian radical literary critic and exponent of Westernism. In 1847 he wrote a letter to Nikolai Vasilevich Gogol (1809-1852), one of Russia's most famous writers and the author of *Dead Souls* and other works which satirized and criticized Russian social conditions. In the letter (which could not be published until many years later, but which became widely known among the Russian intelligentsia), Belinsky condemned Gogol for having forsaken his earlier liberalism, for extolling the autocracy and the Russian Orthodox Church, and for justifying existing institutions (in Gogol's *Selected Passages from Correspondence with Friends*, translated by Jesse Zeldin: Nashville, Tenn., 1969). Belinsky's letter became the credo of Russian radicalism.

4. Count Sergei Semenovich Uvarov (1786-1855) was a prominent educator, President of the Imperial Academy of Sciences, and Minister of Public Instruction from 1833 to 1849. Brilliant and well-educated, he was also a pliable servant of both Alexander I and Nicholas I, and had no difficulty in accommodating himself to the changing policies of the autocracy. It was Uvarov who formulated the doctrine of "Official Nationality," stating that the goal of the Ministry of Public Instruction ought to be to foster a "warm faith in the truly Russian conservative principles of Orthodoxy, Autocracy, and Nationality — which are the last anchor of our salvation and the truest pledge of the strength and greatness of our Fatherland."

5. The privately-owned serfs in the Baltic provinces (Estland, Courland, and Livonia) had been emancipated, with the approval of the Baltic nobility, during the period 1811-1819. Because these former serfs were granted only personal freedom and *not* land, however, their emancipation generally led to a deterioration of their economic condition. Alexander I apparently intended the emancipation of the Baltic peasantry to serve as a "pilot project" for a more general program of emancipation of Russian serfs, and asked Arakcheev to draw up such a plan in 1818. Nothing came of it, however.

6. In 1835, following an outbreak of peasant unrest, Nicholas established a secret committee to investigate the improvement of the lot of the peasantry. The committee recommended that serfs be legally emancipated but not receive land (a proposal similar to the reform undertaken in the Baltic provinces by Alexander I). No action was taken, however. Instead, Nicholas decided to deal with the state peasants alone, and on the recommendation of General Paul Dmitrievich Kiselev (see below) he established a new Ministry of State Domains in 1837, with Kiselev as minister, which oversaw all matters relating to the administration of state peasants and the land they tilled. The new ministry, seeking to standardize the administration of state lands as a precondition to economic improvement, operated on the basis of a complex network of local and provincial officials. The ministry, which has been called "an embryonic Ministry of Agriculture," also dealt with matters of public welfare for the state peasants (for example, it organized health facilities and primary schools) and fostered agricultural improvements on state lands (through agricultural exhibits and the introduction of new farming techniques). Despite the improvements, the deficiencies of the Russian bureaucracy and the resistance to change by the peasants combined to limit the effects of the reform.

7. As military governor of the Danubian principalities of Moldavia and Wallachia after the war of 1828-1829, General P.D. Kiselev (1788-1872) had introduced a number of successful reforms in administration and agriculture. A member of Nicholas I's "secret committee" of 1835, he favored real betterment of the condition of the peasantry. In 1836 Nicholas appointed him head of a special Fifth Section of His Majesty's Chancery, to deal with the state peasants and state lands, and when Nicholas founded the new Ministry of State Domains in 1837 (on Kiselev's advice), Kiselev became its first minister. Kiselev also hoped to introduce reforms to raise the standard of living of privately-owned serfs as well, and proposed the extension of the law of 1803 on "free cultivators" which would grant the peasants personal freedom and *use* of considerable land (which would, however, still be owned by the landlords), clearly define the obligation of the peasants toward the landowners, and allow peasants to purchase land. The proposal met with strong opposition, and a much watered-down version, accepted in 1842, was introduced on a strictly voluntary basis as concerned the landowners.

8. Count Egor Frantsovich Kankrin (1774-1845) was a German by birth (his original name was Krebs), and entered Russian service in 1797. After serving in a variety of economic and military posts, he rose to the rank of general and also served as Minister of Finance (from 1823-1844). Although a strong advocate of protective tariffs, which brought in much-needed revenues, he was opposed to industrialization and the building of railroads, viewing Russia as an essentially agrarian country unable to compete with foreign enterprise. Kankrin did foster technical and commercial education, as did the Ministers of War and Public Instruction in this period. He also attempted, unsuccessfully, to stabilize Russia's monetary system.

9. Evgeny Viktorovich Tarle (1875-1955) was a major Russian historian whose works dealt primarily with the history of France, international relations, and pre-Revolutionary foreign policy. Although in disgrace as a "bourgeois" historian in the 1930s, he became the subject of praise during World War II and was awarded the Stalin Prize three times.

CHAPTER IV

1. Alexander Vasilevich Suvorov (1730-1800) was an outstanding Russian general who played a significant role in the Seven Years War and in the wars against the Turks, as well as in the Italian and Swiss campaigns against Napoleon. Famed throughout Europe as a military commander and hero, Suvorov developed tactics based upon the principles of bold attack and rapid movements of troops. In 1942, during World War II, the Soviet Union began to award a special military decoration for bravery named for Suvorov.

2. Vera Sergeevna Aksakova was the author of a diary which was published after her death: *Dnevnik (1854-1855)* , St. Petersburg, 1913.

3. His Majesty's Own Chancery was founded originally as a bureau which would deal with affairs requiring the emperor's personal participation and which would supervise the execution of his orders. The Chancery quickly expanded, however. In 1826 a Second Section, or Department, was added to deal with the codification of laws,

and the Third Section was added to administer the newly-formed Corps of Gendarmes. Two years later, a Fourth Section was established to administer the philanthropic and educational institutions supported by the Dowager Empress Maria Fedorovna. In 1836 a Fifth Section was created to oversee the reform of the state peasantry; this section subsequently was replaced by the Ministry of State Domains. And in 1843 the Sixth Section was founded and charged with drafting an administrative plan for the Transcaucasian region. Throughout his rule, the Chancery served as a vital instrument of Nicholas's personal policy, by-passing normal state channels. Together with the various secret committees formed by Nicholas on an *ad hoc* basis, the Chancery contributed to the breakdown of the regular order of governmental institutions.

4. Russian laws had not been codified since the *Ulozhenie* (Law Code) of 1649, and had become hopelessly confused and contradictory. The task of codification was entrusted to the Second Section of His Majesty's Own Chancery and in 1833, under the leadership of Speransky (see below), a "Complete Collection of Laws of the Russian Empire," containing all enactments from 1649 to 1830, and a code of currently operative laws were issued. The Code, which modernized Russian laws, remained in effect, with some modifications, until the Bolshevik Revolution.

5. Count Michael Mikhailovich Speransky (1772-1839) was one of the leading statesmen of the reign of Alexander I. He was responsible for administrative reforms (such as the establishment of ministries) in the early nineteenth century and worked out far-reaching plans for the modernization of the Russian government which, however, were not enacted. The victim of political intrigue and the object of jealousy on the part of court circles resentful of his intimacy with Alexander I, Speransky (the low-born son of a village priest), was banished from the capital in 1812. In 1819 he was appointed Governor-General of Siberia and there he carried out meaningful reforms. Returning to St. Petersburg, he subsequently supervised the codification of Russian laws (completed in 1833), perhaps the most important and lasting contribution of his long political career.

6. The Dowager Empress Maria Fedorovna, Nicholas's mother, was very actively involved in philanthropic and educational projects, including a series of girls' schools, orphanages, hospitals and the like.

7

After her death in 1828, these institutions were administered by the Fourth Section of His Majesty's Own Chancery.

7. The *Oprichnina* was the territory set apart from the regular administration of the state by Tsar Ivan the Terrible in 1565, for the purpose of breaking the power of his real or supposed domestic enemies. In these territories, which were mostly confiscated lands, the tsar ruled directly and harshly, aided by *oprichniki*, who carried out a reign of terror. Although officially ended in 1572, the effects of the *oprichnina* were felt long after, for it had aggravated seriously the domestic social and economic crisis within the Russian state.

8. Countess Nesselrode, the wife of Count Karl Robert Nesselrode, had been born Maria Dmitrievna Gureva, the daughter of Count Dmitry Aleksandrovich Gurev, Alexander I's Minister of Finance.

9. Michael Nikiforovich Katkov (1818-1887) was a prominent conservative thinker and publicist in the second half of the nineteenth century. A professor of philosophy at Moscow University, he was best known as a publisher and editor of the newspaper *Moskovskie Vedomosti* (Moscow News) and the monthly journal *Russkii Vestnik* (Russian Herald), both of which were influential organs of opinion. Although he favored progressive economic reforms, Katkov became a leader of conservative nationalist sentiments.

10. The Slavophiles were a Russian philosophical group which, together with their ideological opponents, the Westernizers, became a dominant force in Russian intellectual life in the 1840s. Critical of the "westernization" of Russia since the time of Peter the Great, they called for a return to native Russian traditions and institutions, which they believed embodied principles of harmony, unity, and peace (in contrast to the strife and dissension found in the "false" foundations of Western society). Religious in orientation, the Slavophiles believed in the superiority and historic mission of Russia. Although frequently depicted as conservatives, their criticism of the government was, in fact, quite radical, for they were completely at odds with the governmental policies of "westernization" and "modernization."

11. Michael Petrovich Pogodin (1800-1875) was a journalist and historian noted for his extreme nationalism. A Pan-Slav, he believed

that Russia had been divinely ordained to carry out an important historical mission. A professor at Moscow University, he was associated closely with the so-called "official school" of Russian historiography, which staunchly supported the policies of Nicholas I. His major historical work was the seven-volume *Early History of Russia.*

CHAPTER V

1. Count Karl Robert Nesselrode (1780-1862) served both Alexander I and Nicholas I as Minister of Foreign Affairs. The son of a German who had entered Russian service, Nesselrode rose rapidly in the diplomatic corps, partly because of his willing submission to the desires and outlook of his sovereign. (Metternich said of Nesselrode: "If he were a fish, he would be carried away with the current.") A staunch conservative and legitimist, he is generally felt to have had little substantive effect upon Russian foreign policy.

2. Freiherr vom Stein (1757-1831), one-time Prussian cabinet minister until dismissed on Napoleon's orders, was a German nationalist and liberal reformer. He served as an advisor to Alexander I on German affairs and looked to Russia to aid in the liberation and unification of Germany.

3. Count John Capodistrias (1776-1831) was a native of the Ionian Islands who entered Russian diplomatic service in 1809. He served as a Russian delegate at the Congress of Vienna and shared the duties of Minister of Foreign Affairs with Nesselrode from 1816 to 1822. An ardent advocate of the cause of Greek independence, in 1827 he became the first president of Greece.

4. Prince Francis Xavier Lubecki (1779-1846) served as Polish Minister of Finance from 1821 to 1830. An able administrator and financial expert, he introduced new taxes, encouraged new industries, and strengthened the banking system. Although he contributed much to the economic modernization of Poland, his support of a policy of cooperation with Russia was unpopular with those patriotic Poles who turned increasingly to radical nationalism.

5. Field Marshal Ivan Fedorovich Paskevich (1782-1856) was a military

hero who had led the successful Russian campaign in the Caucasus. He was commander-in-chief of the Russian forces which suppressed the Polish revolt of 1830-1831. Rewarded for his victory with the title of "Prince of Warsaw," he was appointed Viceroy of Poland. His repressive policies only contributed to the growth of Polish nationalism.

6. At the Congress of Vienna in 1815, the Polish city of Cracow was declared to be "free." In 1846, however, after the city witnessed a struggle between rival Polish revolutionary factions and was occupied by Russian troops, it was annexed by Austria with the consent of the other major European powers, including Russia (which had viewed the existence of a "free" part of Poland as a seedbed of unrest in Russian Poland).

7. Count Charles Pozzo di Borgo (1764-1842), a Corsican by birth, entered Russian service in 1803. A bitter enemy of Napoleon, he left Russian service in 1807 in protest against the Treaty of Tilsit, but returned, upon Alexander I's request, in 1812, when Russia resumed the war against France. After 1815 he served as Russian ambassador in Paris.

CHAPTER VI

1. Mehmet-Ali, Pasha of Egypt, was a resourceful and ambitious Ottoman governor. He developed a modern army, stabilized his realm's finances, and added significant new territories (including Crete, the Sudan, and part of Arabia). In 1831 Mehmet-Ali rebelled against the Sultan, and his armies (led by his capable son, Ibrahim) conquered much of Syria and threatened Constantinople itself. When Britain refused to come to his aid, the Sultan desperately appealed to Russia for assistance. Nonetheless, despite Russian help, the Ottomans were obliged to cede Syria and other territories to Egypt, in the Convention of Kutahia.

2. In the conversations with Lord Aberdeen in England in 1844 and again in those with Sir Hamilton Seymour in St. Petersburg in 1853, Nicholas I apparently believed he had gained the tacit acceptance by Great Britain of the need for a partition of the Ottoman Empire when that state collapsed, an event Nicholas regarded as imminent.

3. The Russo-Turkish Treaty of Unkiar-Skelessi was signed in 1833, as the result of Russian assistance to the Sultan in the latter's struggle with his rebellious vassal, Mehmet-Ali. The treaty was more than an alliance, however, for Turkey pledged that, if Russia requested, the Porte would close the Straits to all foreign warships. Although the Russians viewed the treaty as a defensive one, other governments (especially England) regarded it as an attempt to transform Turkey into a Russian satellite.

CHAPTER VII

1. Michael Aleksandrovich Bakunin (1814-1876) was a Russian revolutionary leader, anarchist theoretician, and Marx's rival in the First International.

2. Count Peter Aleksandrovich Valuev (1814-1890) served as Minister of the Interior (1861-1868) and Chairman of the Committee of Ministers (1877-1881). He played an active part in the preparation of the Great Reforms of the reign of Alexander II (especially the emancipation of the serfs and the establishment of the *zemstvo* system of local self-government). His diary, covering political events from 1847 to 1884, is a valuable source of information about the policies and personalities of Imperial Russia in the nineteenth century.

3. Sevastopol, a major Crimean naval base and port on the Black Sea (at Sevastopol Bay) was the site of a famous siege (1854-1855) in the Crimean War. The city was heavily damaged in the final assault on it in September, 1855, which cost both sides heavy casualties.

4. Alexander Nikolaevich Benois (1870-1960) was an eminent Russian painter, theatrical designer, art historian and critic. Along with Sergei Diaghilev, he played an important part in familiarizing the Russian public with Western artistic trends and in acquainting Western Europeans with the works of Russian artists, musicians, and ballet companies. Benois' study to which Presniakov refers is an article entitled "Dvortsovoe stroitelstvo Imperatora Nikolaia I" [The Palace Construction of Emperor Nicholas I], *Starye gody*, July-September, 1913 (author's reference).

5. K. A. Thon was a favorite architect of Nicholas I, noted chiefly for his churches, which were supposed to be based upon native Russian models. Although his buildings are widely regarded as lackluster, he did contribute to the study of Russian antiquity, a characteristic feature of the reign of Nicholas I.

6. A lady-in-waiting at the Court, Mlle. Nelidova became the mistress of Nicholas I – a fact widely known to many, including the empress. Count Peter Andreevich Kleinmichael, an unpopular and unpleasant official, acted as intermediary between Nicholas and Nelidova, adopted their children, and rose to a position of prominence in the latter part of Nicholas's reign.

7. Nicholas Petrovich Poggenpohl (1824-1894) was the editor of *Le Nord*, a semi-official organ of the Russian government which he established in Brussels in 1856. From 1859 *Le Nord* included a special section on the question of the emancipation of the serfs. M. P. Pogodin, P.A. Valuev, and other important Russian writers and statesmen published in *Le Nord*. Poggenpohl was also the author of *La Paix ou la Guerre, ou La Russie en 1863, lettres politiques par N. de Poggenpohl* (Paris, 1863).

8. N. S. Shtakelberg, "Zagadka smerti Nikolai I" [The Mystery of the Death of Nicholas I], *Russkoe Proshloe*, I (1923) (author's footnote).

SUGGESTIONS FOR FURTHER READING

There is no scholarly, up-to-date English-language biography of Nicholas I. The most complete, though scarcely definitive, study of Nicholas's life and reign presently available in English is Constantin de Grunwald's *Tsar Nicholas I* (London, 1954; New York, 1955), a translation by Brigit Patmore of the original French version, *La Vie de Nicolas Ier* (Paris, 19-46). Other biographical studies in Western languages worth consulting are Paul Lacroix, *Histoire de la vie et du regne de Nicolas Ier* (Paris, 1868); the valuable and heavily-documented *Geschichte Russlands unter Kaiser Nikolaus I.* (4 vols., Berlin, 1904-1909) by Theodor Schiemann; and J.H. Schnitzler, *Histoire intime de la Russie sous les empereurs Alexandre et Nicolas et particulierement pedant la crise de 1825* (2 vols., Paris, 1847), also published in English translation as *Secret History of the Court and Government of Russia under Alexander the First and the Emperor Nicholas* (2 vols., London, 1854). An illuminating view of Nicholaevan Russia is further provided by the classic *La Russie en 1839* by Astolphe de Custine (4 vols., Brussels, 1843), an abridged translation of which appeared under the title *Journey for our Time* (New York, 1952). Custine's insights and prophecies are evaluated in B. Hopper's "Custine and Russia—A Century After," *American Historical Review*, LVII (1952) and in George F. Kennan, *The Marquis de Custine and His Russia in 1839* (Princeton, 1971).

Russian officialdom in the reign of Nicholas I has begun to receive significant scholarly attention. Of particular value are Walter M. Pintner's provocative article, "The Social Characteristics of the Early Nineteenth Century Russian Bureaucracy," *Slavic Review,* Vol. 29, No. 3 (September, 1970), pp. 429-443; Sidney Monas's essay, "Bureaucracy in Russia under Nicholas I," in Michael Cherniavsky (ed.), *The Structure of Russian History* (New York, 1970), pp. 269-281; and Hans J. Torke, "Das russische Beamtentum in der ersten Halfte des 19. Jahrhunderts" in *Forschungen zur osteuropaischen Geschichte*, Band 13 (1967), pp. 7-345. An outstanding study of one of the key political figures of the reigns of Alexander I and Nicholas I is Marc Raeff, *Michael Speransky: Statesman of Imperial Russia* (The Hague, 1957). The political police has been the subject of two recent works: Sidney Monas, *The Third Section* (Cambridge, Mass., 1961) and the more heavily documented volume by P.S. Squire, *The Third Department: The Political Police in the Russia of Nicholas I* (London and New York, 1968). The Russian army, as a military force and as a significant reflection of and influence upon Russian society, has been treated thoughtfully in John S. Curtiss, *The Russian Army under Nicholas I, 1825-1855* (Durham, N.C., 1965). Other institutional aspects have been examined in Samuel Kucherov's article, "Administration of Justice under Nicholas I of Russia," *American Slavic and East European Review*, Vol. 7, No. 2 (April, 1948), pp. 125-138; and in Roderick E. McGrew, *Russia and the Cholera, 1823-1832* (Madison, 1965), which focuses upon the government's ability to respond to a major national crisis.

Two indispensable studies of Russian economic life in this period are Walter M. Pintner, *Russian Economic Policy under Nicholas I* (Ithaca, 1967) and William L. Blackwell, *The Beginnings of Russian Industrialization, 1800-1860* (Princeton, 1968). Also see Olga Crisp, "The State Peasants under Nicholas I," *Slavonic Review*, Vol. 37, No. 89 (June, 1959), pp. 387-412; and Richard Haywood, *The Beginnings of Railway Development in Russia in the Reign of Nicholas I, 1835-1842* (Durham, N.C., 1969).

Russian diplomacy in the reign of Nicholas I, especially in the matter of the Eastern Question, has received considerable scholarly attention. The classic works for this period remain Vernon Puryear, *England, Russia and the Straits Question, 1844-1856* (Berkeley, 1931), and Philip E. Mosely, *Russian Diplomacy and the Opening of the Eastern Question in 1838 and 1839* (Cambridge, Mass., 1934). J.A.R. Marriott, *The Eastern Question* (Oxford, 1951), M.S. Anderson, *The Eastern Question, 1774-1923* (London, 1966), and A.J.P. Taylor, *The Struggle for Mastery in Europe, 1848-1914* (Oxford, 1954) provide more general narratives.

Also useful are G.H. Bolsover, "Nicholas I and the Partition of Turkey," *Slavonic Review,* Vol. 27, No. 68 (December, 1948), pp. 115-145, and Harold Temperley, *England and the Near East: The Crimea* (London, 1936). A recent popular account is Peter Gibbs, *Crimean Blunder* (New York, 1960). A convenient guide to the controversies surrounding the war itself is given by Brison Gooch, "A Century of Historiography on the Origins of the Crimean War," *American Historical Review,* LXII (October, 1956), pp. 33-58.

Other aspects of Russian foreign policy during Nicholas's rule are covered in A. Lobanov-Rostovsky, *Russia and Europe, 1825-1878* (Ann Arbor, 1954) and Barbara Jelavich, *Russia and Greece During the Regency of King Otton, 1832-1835* (Thessalonika, 1962). Nicholas I's confrontation with the supranational forces of revolution and nationalism are discussed in Isaiah Berlin's "1848 and Russia," *Slavonic and East European Review,* Vol. 26, No. 67 (April, 1948), pp. 341-360; Oscar J. Hammer, "Free Europe Versus Russia, 1830-1854," *American Slavic and East European Review,* Vol. 11, No. 1 (February, 1952), pp. 27-41; Eugene Horvath, "Russia and the Hungarian Revolution (1848-1849)," *Slavonic Review,* Vol. 17, No. 36 (April, 1934), pp. 628-643; and R. F. Leslie, *Polish Politics and the Revolution of November, 1830* (London, 1956).

The doctrines of "Official Nationality" which so thoroughly permeated Nicholas's regime are described, in terms of their ideological content and the men who attempted to put them into practice, in Nicholas V. Riasanovsky, *Nicholas I*

and Official Nationality in Russia, 1825-1855 (Berkeley, 1959).
Also see L. Strakhovsky, *L'Empereur Nicolas I et l'esprit na-
tionale russe* (Louvain, 1928).

The Decembrist revolt of 1825, with which Nicholas's
reign began so dramatically, is the subject of Anatole G. Ma-
zour, *The First Russian Revolution, 1825* (Berkeley, 1937);
M. Zetlin, *The Decembrists* (New York, 1958); and Marc
Raeff, *The Decembrist Movement* (Englewood Cliffs, N.J.,
1966), which also provides English translations of numerous
Russian primary sources. The conservative side of the political spectrum is discussed in Richard Pipes, "Karamzin's Conception of Monarchy," *Harvard Slavic Studies,* IV (1957),
pp. 35-58.

Other intellectual and political currents have also received scholarly attention. The serialized essay by Isaiah Berlin,
"A Marvelous Decade, 1838-1848: The Birth of the Russian
Intelligentsia," *Encounter,* IV-VI (1955-1956), is especially
successful in capturing the atmosphere of the intellectual circles of that era. An outstanding intellectual biography of a
key figure in the history of the Russian intelligentsia is Mar-
tin Malia, *Alexander Herzen and the Birth of Russian Social-
ism* (Cambridge, Mass., 1961). Other political trends are discussed in G. Sourine, *Le Fourierisme en Russie* (Paris, 1936);
Frederick I. Kaplan, "Russian Fourierism of the 1840's," *American Slavic and East European Review,* Vol. 17, No. 2 (April, 1958), pp. 161-172; Edward J. Brown, *Stankevich and His
Moscow Circle, 1830-1840* (Stanford, 1966); and two old, but
still valuable, studies by E.H. Carr: *The Romantic Exiles*
(London, 1933) and *Michael Bakunin* (New York, 1937). A general summary of these currents is provided by Michael Florin-
sky, "Russian Social and Political Thought, 1825-1855," *Russian Review,* Vol. 6, No. 2 (Spring, 1947), pp. 77-85.

Major philosophical currents in Nicholas's reign are treat-
ed in Nicholas V. Riasanovsky, *Russia and the West in the
Teaching of the Slavophiles* (Cambridge, Mass., 1952); Peter
K. Christoff, *An Introduction to Nineteenth Century Russian*

Slavophilism: A Study in Ideas. A.S. Khomiakov (The Hague,
1961); A. Gratieux, *A.S. Khomiakov et le mouvement slavo-
phile* (2 vol., Paris, 1939); E. Chmielewski, *Tribune of the
Slavophiles: Konstantin Aksakov* (Gainesville, Fla., 1961);
Charles Quenet, *Tchaadaev et les lettres philosophiques* (Paris, 1931); Abbott Gleason, *European and Muscovite: Ivan
Kireevsky and the Origins of Slavophilism* (Cambridge, Mass.,
1972); and, less satisfactorily, E. Moskoff, *The Russian Philo-
sopher Chaadaev: His Ideas and His Epoch* (New York, 1937).
English-language translations of some of Chaadaev's most important writings are provided by Raymond T. McNally, *Major
Works of Peter Chaadaev* (Notre Dame, 1969); and by Mary-
Barbara Zeldin, *Philosophical Letters and Apology of a Mad-
man* (Knoxville, Tenn., 1969).

   Biographical data on other significant writers and think-
ers may be found in H. Bowman, *Vissarion Belinskii: A Study
in the Origins of Social Criticism in Russia* (Cambridge, Mass.,
1954); Richard Hare, *Pioneers of Russian Social Thought*
(2nd., rev., New York, 1964); and in Anthony G. Cross, *N.
M. Karamzin: A Study of His Literary Career, 1783-1803*
(Carbondale and Edwardsville, Ill., 1971) which, despite its
title, also deals with Karamzin's later activity and his role as
a political thinker and historian.

Presniakov, Aleksandr Evgen'evich, 1870-1929
  Emperor Nicholas I of Russia: the apogee of autocracy, 1825-
1855 [by] A.E. Presniakov. Ed. and trans. by Judith C. Zacek.
With "Nicholas I and the course of Russian history" by Nicholas
V. Riasanovsky. [Gulf Breeze, Fla.] Academic International
Press, 1974.
  xl, 102 p. illus. 23 cm. (The Russian series, v. 23)
  Translation of Apogei samoderzhaviia (title romanized)
  "Notes": p. 80-97; "Suggestions for further reading": p. 98-102.

  1. Russia—Hist.—Nicholas I, 1825-1855. 2. Nicholas I, Emperor
of Russia, 1796-1855. I. Zacek, Judith C., ed. and tr. II. Riasanovsky, Nicholas Valentine, 1923-   . Nicholas I and the course of
Russian history. III. Title.

DK210.P713   947.070924   73-90779
ISBN: 0-87569-053-X